THE ASTRONAUT'S WIFE

THE ASTRONAUT'S WIFE

HOW LAUNCHING MY HUSBAND INTO OUTER SPACE
CHANGED THE WAY I LIVE ON EARTH

STACEY MORGAN

Visit Tyndale online at tyndale.com.

Visit Tyndale Momentum online at tyndalemomentum.com.

Visit Stacey Morgan at staceymorgan2000.com.

Tyndale, Tyndale's quill logo, Tyndale Momentum, and the Tyndale Momentum logo are registered trademarks of Tyndale House Ministries. Tyndale Momentum is a nonfiction imprint of Tyndale House Publishers, Carol Stream, Illinois.

Designed by Dean H. Renninger

The author is represented by the literary agency of Alive Literary Agency, www.aliveliterary.com.

For information about special discounts for bulk purchases, please contact Tyndale House Publishers at csresponse@tyndale.com, or call 1-855-277-9400.

Library of Congress Cataloging-in-Publication Data

A catalog record for this book is available from the Library of Congress.

ISBN 978-1-4964-5462-1 (hc)
ISBN 978-1-4964-5463-8 (sc)

Printed in the United States of America

28 27 26 25 24 23 22
7   6   5   4   3   2   1

To my fellow military and astronaut spouses—
the most courageous and resilient people I know.

You always find a way to thrive in the most challenging seasons.
Never forget that you are a critical part of every mission's success.

CONTENTS

FOREWORD

BY ANNIE F. DOWNS

I have the best seat in this story. I walked into Stacey's life by walking into the Johnson Space Center. I was in Houston for an event, and Stacey met some friends and me for a tour of NASA. I have always been very into space and space travel, so getting to meet an astronaut's wife and tour with her felt like such a huge deal. Within minutes, we were seeing the International Space Station and hearing Drew's voice from outer space.

Stacey and I became fast friends that day over burgers at lunch and laughs as we went from place to place at NASA while I kept asking if I could hop in her car for a ride between stops. We exchanged phone numbers, not knowing that our friendship was beginning literally days before the world would shut down due to COVID and we would all be secluded in our homes. I got to jump into this story right as Drew was headed home and right as Stacey's life was about to change again.

That's when she started to write it all down—all this season had been, all her life with Drew had been, and all that was to come. And the story changed for me—from living it with her,* to feeling it deep

---

* A lot of the times Stacey mentions watching Netflix, I was co-watching the same shows from across the country, across the pandemic—alone as well. It was a gift. We laughed a lot.

in my own life and seeing how her story reminded me of God and my story too.

I heard an interviewer say recently that the highest compliment you can pay someone who has put a book out into the world is to say you've been moved by their memoir—whether you know the author or not. I agree with that; Stacey is such a fine writer and storyteller that you will feel connected whether or not you are friends with her. It's rare that we get an inside look at such a public job, one we have watched movies about and read books about and, looking up into the sky, wondered about. When I finished reading this book, I felt more appreciation for family, for friendship, for sacrifice, and for God's caring hand.

Stories about outer space remind us that God is so much bigger than we can imagine. But stories of family, of connection, of figuring out the hard times and walking through them together remind us that God is, at the same time, personal and intimate and caring. He is all these things, and I'm thankful for the way Stacey masterfully weaves that truth into these stories of an astronaut's wife.

You are about to embark on one of the most unique journeys I've ever seen with one of the funniest, kindest, and best guides around. As you read, may God meet you in your own story in ways that are—forgive me—out of this world.

EVERYTHING I NEEDED TO KNOW ABOUT SPACE I LEARNED FROM TOM HANKS

The first time I watched a rocket launch, I was sitting on the hard linoleum floor of my elementary school cafeteria. After herding all the fifth graders into the large empty room, our teachers told us to sit quietly and keep our hands to ourselves. The lunch ladies were noisily preparing our noontime meal behind the kitchen doors, and the smell of chicken patties and tater tots wafted into the room. Once all the students were seated, Miss Farrell walked solemnly to the front of the room and turned on a boxy television strapped to the top of a wheeled cart. A live shot of space shuttle *Discovery* flickered onto the screen, the white spaceship and its bright orange fuel tank a beautiful contrast to the sunny blue sky. As the countdown neared, my friend elbowed me, signaling me to look over at our teacher, who was sniffling loudly into a tissue. The other teachers stood by nervously wringing their hands, their eyes glued to the TV screen. As ten-year-olds, we didn't understand the adults' emotional response, but we applauded loudly when *Discovery* successfully lifted off the launchpad and rocketed into the sky in an impressive plume of fire and smoke. Then we filed back to our classrooms, sat down at our desks, and counted the minutes until recess.

It wasn't until years later that I began to understand the historical and emotional significance of that day. I know now that the launch I watched at school in September 1988 was the first for NASA since the 1986 *Challenger* disaster, which, at the time, was the deadliest accident in the US space program's history. *Challenger's* boosters exploded just after liftoff, claiming the lives of all seven astronauts on board, including teacher Christa McAuliffe. America watched the fiery blast in shock and then fell into a state of shared grief. Now over two years later, it wasn't surprising that my teachers cried that day in the cafeteria—*Discovery's* safe launch marked America's triumphant "Return to Flight" and the end of our collective mourning period.

After that, I maintained a peripheral view of the US space program at best. In history class, I studied the Cold War and how the "space race" to the moon between America and the Soviet Union was just one of many battles between these two world superpowers. I vaguely recall seeing the televised coverage of subsequent shuttle launches from Florida's Kennedy Space Center on my rabbit-eared television. But if I'm honest, most of my limited understanding of space history came from watching Tom Hanks in the movie *Apollo 13*.

All that changed in 2012 when my husband came home from work one day in an uncharacteristically giddy mood. "NASA has opened up the application window for a new class of astronauts," Drew told me with a level of excitement usually reserved for Christmas morning. I was genuinely puzzled. Why was he telling me this? Drew was an Army officer and medical doctor dedicated to his profession, so I didn't see the relevance of his announcement. Not only that, but while I didn't know much about NASA, I had heard that the shuttle program was scheduled to end within the year, so why were they still hiring astronauts? What vehicle would they even fly on?

"Well," I said in an attempt to share equally random news, "chicken was on sale at the commissary today."

"No, you don't get it," Drew said as he stepped forward and grasped my hand. "I want to apply to be in the next class of NASA astronauts."

"Um, what?" I asked with a look that must have been equal parts confusion and horror. We had a plan for our future, and Drew becoming an astronaut was certainly not in it. We loved the Army. We were dedicated to the Special Operations community. To thrive in that stressful world, you have to be all in, and we were in deep. Even our four kids, ages two to nine, accepted Drew's frequent absences as part of their normal life rhythm. As far as I knew, military life was our past, present, and future.

"Look, don't freak out," Drew said. "NASA has never selected an Army doctor before. The likelihood of my being chosen is very small, but I want to try. Okay?"

"Okaaay," I said, clinging to the 99 percent chance he wouldn't be chosen and we wouldn't have to throw our family's well-scripted plans out the window.

"No matter what, I'll always be able to say I was a NASA applicant," Drew joked. "I doubt I'll even make it through the first round."

Except he *did* make it through the first round, and the next, and the next. The application process eventually culminated in a life-changing phone call in June 2013. During that conversation, NASA invited Drew into the twenty-first class of NASA astronauts, upended our lives, and transformed me into an amateur space historian.

Initially, I was embarrassed by how little I knew about the American space program. Never one to go into something blind, I read a handful of books and watched movies like *The Right Stuff* to help fill the significant gaps in my knowledge.

Like many people, I had only a vague understanding of the US space program's dynamic beginnings. I learned that the National Aeronautics and Space Administration (NASA) was established in 1958, and only three years later, President John F. Kennedy made the audacious pledge to put Americans on the moon by the end of the decade. Three programs—Mercury, Gemini, and then Apollo— brought the US ever closer to that visionary goal in less than ten years. The speed with which the programs developed, combined with the unbelievable bravery of those early astronauts, is staggering. When *Apollo 11*'s lunar lander touched down on the moon's surface on July 20, 1969, the world held its breath. And when Neil Armstrong said those famous words "That's one small step for man, one giant leap for mankind," the world cheered.[1] It was a monumental accomplishment and a testament to humankind's ingenuity to push the boundaries of our own existence.

America's lunar initiative ended after *Apollo 17*'s final mission to the moon surface in 1972. However, one of the Apollo program's lesser-known legacies occurred in 1975, when an American crew docked their Apollo capsule with a Soviet Soyuz capsule while in orbit around the Earth. The literal joining of the two spaceships became a powerful symbol of the fact that Americans and Soviets could work together as allies in exploration, even though they remained geopolitical enemies.

Over the next decade, NASA's focus shifted, and they began imagining a future in which American astronauts could live and work in space. That led to the development of a brand-new type of spaceship, the space shuttle.

When the first shuttle launched in 1981, it sparked a massive flurry of American interest in space exploration and created a huge opportunity for international partnerships. The space shuttle fleet, consisting of *Columbia, Challenger, Discovery, Atlantis,* and *Endeavour,* flew 135 missions, carried astronauts from sixteen different countries, docked with the Soviet space station Mir, and deployed the Hubble Space Telescope. But its lasting legacy would be its commission to haul the components for the International Space Station (ISS) into orbit.[2]

Starting in 1998, a multinational team of astronauts and cosmonauts (the Russian term for *astronauts*) built the largest and most complex spaceship ever devised. From its outset, the ISS was as much a wonder of international relationships as it was a technological marvel. The station was purposely designed so that its full operation is possible only in full cooperation with our international partners, most notably our intermittent frenemies, the Russians.[3]

After the last space shuttle launch, many Americans assumed that NASA closed up shop and locked its doors. At least, that's what I thought. Gone were the days of smiling astronauts in bright orange space suits and televised launch countdowns from Florida. So when Drew told me that NASA was not only still hiring astronauts but somehow still launching them into outer space to live and work on the ISS, I was intrigued. How were they doing it? You may be as surprised as I was to learn that we were hitching rides on Russian rockets.

If thinking about US space history rekindles a small flame of hazy memories in your mind, learning about the Russian space program is like gazing into a fascinating parallel universe. Unlike America's program, the Soviet space program was cloaked in secrecy, and much of its early history was not known to Westerners until the Soviet Union fell in the early 1990s. In fact, the Soviets established their base of space operations 1,300 miles southeast of Moscow at the Baikonur

Cosmodrome complex in Kazakhstan, a former Soviet republic known for its nomadic culture, freezing winters, and blistering summers. The Soviets built their remote, secret spaceport and the surrounding support city for one sole purpose—to launch rockets. It's about as far a cry from bustling, colorful, coastal Florida as a person can get.

The opening move in the US-Soviet space race was the successful launch of the mysterious *Sputnik 1*, the first space satellite, from the Baikonur Cosmodrome. On subsequent missions, the Soviets launched the first dog, Laika; the first man, Yuri Gagarin; and the first woman, Valentina Tereshkova. This string of "firsts" fueled the space race rivalry with the United States and paved the way for Soyuz, Apollo's competitor in the sprint to the lunar surface. After the Americans landed on the moon first, the Soviet Soyuz mission was abruptly changed, but the vehicle was not. While there have been many technological upgrades over the years, the size, shape, and soul of the Soyuz spacecraft have remained much the same since the 1960s, as has the spirit of the entire Soyuz program. Every aspect of a Soyuz launch is steeped in history, tradition, and Russian vodka. Almost everything Yuri Gagarin did before his history-making launch from Baikonur in 1961 is still followed to the letter by today's cosmonauts at their own launches. For better or worse, while the Americans began and ended new space programs and processes, the Russians stuck with what worked—a robust and reliable system that has successfully launched cargo and crew into space for over fifty years.

Once the space shuttle program ended in 2011, Soyuz rockets became the only game in town. When we arrived at NASA in 2013, there was little doubt that when Drew was assigned to a mission, he would fly on a Soyuz rocket. And while every American astronaut dreams of launching from US soil, Drew knew that to be a part of Soyuz would mean something so much more than a rocket ride into space. Soyuz is a rich cultural experience that, in many ways, reflects the essence of space exploration—cooperation that transcends historical rivalries in the spirit of discovery, lifelong friendships between astronauts and cosmonauts, and an example of hope for humanity.

That is why the first time I watched a rocket launch in person, I stood, a proud American, on what had once been a top-secret Soviet military base. My husband climbed into his Soyuz rocket on the same launchpad used by the Soviets for *Sputnik 1* in 1957 and Gagarin's launch in 1961. And in what can only be described as an ironic twist of fate, I watched Drew's Russian rocket lift off into the night sky on July 20, 2019, the fiftieth anniversary of the Apollo moon landing. The event was an astonishing confluence of historical events, stunningly intersecting with my own life. On that day, I was not just a witness to history but a part of it.

CHAPTER 1

EVERY ADVENTURE BEGINS AT A CROSSROADS

CHOOSE HOPE OVER FEAR

July 20, 2019

Baikonur Cosmodrome, Kazakhstan

At 9 p.m. on the desert steppe of Kazakhstan, it is still close to 100 degrees outside. My stomach has a knot in it that won't go away, and the bumpy ride across the old Soviet-era roads of the Baikonur Cosmodrome hasn't helped. The four kids and I tumble out of the van and look around, taking in the bizarre, celebratory scene in front of us.

Hundreds of people are milling about, most of them speaking languages I don't know. Many are dressed in full "outer space" gear: The vivid mission patches, NASA logos, and color photos of the crew printed on their T-shirts and hats are bright splashes of color against the dusky evening. A man saunters by in an astronaut costume, complete with a bubble helmet. These spectators have paid thousands of dollars to travel from across the globe for this moment: a chance to see a Soyuz rocket launch, this one with my husband and his two crewmates strapped into the tiny capsule on top.

Despite my nervousness, I turn and smile at my oldest child, Daniel, who is quietly taking it all in. He's a Star Wars fanatic, and a few years before, he might have wanted to be in costume himself. But not now that he's fifteen. He's far too cool, and he knows full well that this is no Hollywood movie.

As the space tourists flow toward the public viewing area on the left, our NASA escort, an experienced astronaut who has flown on Soyuz, guides us to the right. I check for my girls—twelve-year-old Amelia is scanning the crowd for one of her besties, another astronaut's daughter whose dad is also strapped into the rocket we can see in the distance. I'm glad she can share this experience with a friend who gets it. Sophia, my athletic ten-year-old, is bouncing with excitement as she grabs my hand. "Can we swim in the hotel pool again tonight, Mom?"

Sure, honey. Just as soon as we launch your father into space. "We'll see," I say as I put my free arm around Gabriella—she's never one to pass up a cuddle, especially today. At only eight, she has the most questions and worries about her dad leaving.

All four kids accounted for, we keep moving, bypassing the relatively well-lit grandstand area filled with giddy space enthusiasts. Next we pass the gaggle of international press and science reporters who have set up their tripod cameras and portable lights, which sprout like artificial trees growing out of the flat scrub grass. Our group, along with a handful of NASA employees, move into an open spot on the far end of the field. It's darker here, and quiet.

I can hear the reporters speaking into their cameras in preparation for the launch that will begin in less than thirty minutes. One voice in particular cuts through the night. It's a British reporter who is recounting everything that unfolded earlier in the day, with specific emphasis on one of the families she had observed: "And then the children—hoisted up on the shoulders of family and friends—reached out their hands for one last wave, one last touch through the bus windows, one last 'I love you' before the bus with their father and his fellow crewmates pulled away to the launchpad where their Soyuz rocket waits."[4]

She doesn't know that the very family she's telling the world about is standing within earshot. I remember her from earlier in the day. After watching Drew complete the final leak check of his Russian Sokol space suit, the kids and I sat behind a table with a thick glass wall separating us from Drew, who sat behind an identical table on the other side of the glass. The two men who would make the journey into space with him, Italian crewmate Luca Parmitano and Russian cosmonaut commander Aleksandr Skvortsov, sat next to him at the table. The room behind us was full of family and friends of the crew, program officials, and several dozen members of the press who were maneuvering their cameras to get the best angle. The glass was soundproof, so in between me whisper-hissing at the children to "Remember that the cameras are watching so *SIT UP* and *STOP* touching your sister," we used a microphone on the table to broadcast our public goodbyes to Drew through the overhead speakers in the ceiling. Then we stood up, put our hands on the glass, and locked eyes for the last time. Drew mouthed, "I love you," just before turning away and walking out.

The suit-up room emptied quickly as we rushed outside for a spot to watch the crew ceremoniously exit the building and board the bus that would take them to the rocket. After the bus pulled away, everyone—family, official guests, tourists, and press—attempted to make their way back to their own vehicles. During the awkward, accidental mingling that resulted, the British reporter approached us and asked if we were willing to speak to her about the launch. Giving a coherent interview in the midst of this emotional buildup and the jostling crowd seemed impossible, so our escort politely declined on my behalf.

* * *

My real goodbye to Drew had been the night before. My escort walked me to the quarantine facility, only a few hundred yards from our Baikonur hotel, where a silent guard hit the button, allowing the fortified gate to roll open. Once I slipped inside, another escort walked me down the gravel path to a low-slung building recently built by the Russians for just this purpose. It has three simple motel-like rooms, each with a bed, chair, and bathroom. No phone, no TV, no clock radio, no extra frills. But it gave me and Drew the one thing we needed most, a few minutes of privacy—no kids, no doctors, no TV crews. Just us. The last time for a long time.

"I'm sad to leave you," Drew said as we sat next to each other in the quiet room. "Part of me wishes I wasn't going."

"I know," I replied. "This will be the longest we've ever been apart in the twenty years we've been together. I'll miss you so much." My eyes filled with tears, and my chest was heavy.

"You've got this," Drew said, putting his arms around me. "It's another big adventure for us."

"I am proud of you," I said. I leaned in and pressed my face into Drew's chest so he couldn't see the tears running down my cheeks. "And as hard as it is to say goodbye, I'm excited for you. These aren't sad tears; they're happy, proud, excited, and anxious tears. I think the anticipation of tomorrow may be worse than the actual launch."

"I think so too," he said. "I just want to get on that rocket and get this waiting over with."

A couple of hours later, we gathered up the last few personal items of Drew's—uniforms, extra clothes, books, souvenirs—that he wanted me to take home. Then he walked me back to the gate. My escort was waiting on the other side of the fence.

"Good night," Drew said. "I love you."

"Goodbye," I said as we embraced one last time before Drew turned around and headed to his room for one last night on Earth.

* * *

Now, four hours after the prelaunch press conference, the reporter who approached me earlier is the one I can see best, her face illuminated by her camera light, her hand holding a black foam microphone. Behind her, at least half a dozen other reporters are doing similar reporting in Spanish, Italian, and Russian voices. It's as if I've stepped onto a movie set, and we're almost at the climactic scene where the international press will report to the world whether or not the daring and dangerous Earth-saving mission has been successful.

With his medium build, dark hair, and friendly smile, my NASA escort looks and acts precisely how most people imagine an astronaut should. He exudes a quiet confidence acquired from years of training and spaceflight experience. He gently encourages me to move toward the middle of our small section of the field for the best view. He peers at his watch and tells me, "Less than ten minutes until launch." The knot in my stomach grows tighter.

My kids are wandering around, talking to the grandparents, uncles, and friends we brought with us on this epic pilgrimage. I call to them, and they head in my direction, kicking the dusty ground as they walk. My mom is already beside me, while my in-laws stand with Drew's two brothers, nervously chatting and checking their watches and cameras. Our close friends are grouped together but spread out in a line, so they all have a clear view of the launchpad that appears directly in front of us, only about a mile away. By rocket launch standards, we are really close.

"We need to stay together now," I tell the kids. My voice sounds deep and solemn, even to my own ears. "We're going to move up to the front and hold hands while we wait for the launch."

Whether they understand the gravity of the situation or know I'm serious by my tone of voice, I hear none of the usual complaining that comes when told to hold hands with a sibling. My escort hovers behind me at a respectful distance, ready if I need him.

"Two minutes out," he tells me. There are no blaring announcements over a loudspeaker or giant digital countdown clocks like spectators had at the Florida shuttle launches. We just look at our own watches and phones in the dark, knowing that the Russian ground crew will ignite the rocket at exactly 9:28 p.m., not a minute earlier or later.

My fingers tingle as I grip a small, sweaty hand with each of mine; my breathing is shallow and rapid. I take a deep breath to help center myself. If I didn't have the children there with me, I might be tempted to sink to the ground and let the intense feelings of anxiety overwhelm me. But as I glance down to check my own watch, I catch a glimpse of the tattoo peeking out from behind my watchband. It is brand-new, inked only three weeks before. The fancy, slanted script reads "Esther 4:14," a reference to an Old Testament Bible verse that has always spoken to me, but never more than in this moment.

Esther's story has *everything*! A crazy king, a beauty pageant, a reluctant queen, secret identities, dangerous plots, and a particularly gruesome but gratifying ending for the villain. My tattoo references the point in the story when Queen Esther is at a crossroads. Her uncle has told her of a plot to kill their people, the Jews, and he's asking her to *do something*. The verse inked on my wrist is her uncle's response when he senses her hesitation: "Who knows whether you have not come to the kingdom for such a time as this?" (Esther 4:14, ESV).

God placed Esther into a moment of history for a specific purpose, but he gave her the choice of how to respond. Would she choose the path dictated by fear and do nothing? Or would Esther choose the path paved in hope, willing to act and face her fears, confident that God would use the situation, regardless of the outcome, for his greater purpose? Either way, she knew her life would change dramatically, and her decision could prove fatal. Spoiler: Esther decided to step up like a complete boss and declare, "If I perish, I perish" (Esther 4:16, ESV). Man, I wish I had guts like Esther.

Though standing in a hot, dry field on the opposite side of the world waiting for the one-minute countdown to begin pales in comparison to the life-or-death decision this biblical queen faced, in this moment, in my soul, I am Esther. The emotional cocktail of pride, excitement, elation, nervousness, stress, and fear is so potent I feel completely overwhelmed. My mind is filled with unanswerable questions, as I imagine Esther's was. *What if something goes wrong? What if the rocket explodes? Have I just said goodbye forever to my husband of twenty years? What if something happens while he's gone and he can't come home? Will I be able to handle all the logistics and emotional burden of raising four children on my own?* Even with years of training and full confidence in the equipment and technology, things happen, mistakes are made. *On the flip side, even if everything goes perfectly, what comes next? What will life be like with Drew in space and us back here on Earth? Will our relationship suffer? Do I have the skills, support, and endurance I will need for this marathon mission?* I am standing on the edge of a psychological cliff, my toes dangling off the edge, not knowing if in a few short moments I will be filled with the elation of a successful rocket launch or the shocking downward plunge of mourning the loss of my best friend and my children's father. My fear and uncertainty are palpable as I stand at this crossroads, and my heart is pounding like a drum. No matter which way this launch goes, I know that my life, and the lives of my children, will never be the same. Both outcomes are filled with uncertainty and unknowns, the fear of which far outweighs my fear of the rocket launch itself.

"Thirty seconds," a voice calls out from the darkness behind me. We can see the support structures beginning to move on the launchpad.

"Ten seconds."

Whatever happens next, we will choose the path of hope and together face whatever comes next. After all, the fear in my heart is heavy and tight, but it is not unfamiliar.

* * *

June 2007
Southern Pines, North Carolina

It was the height of the War on Terror, and Drew was deployed to Afghanistan. I wasn't alone; the majority of my friends' and neighbors' husbands were deployed as well. Covert and extremely dangerous, their missions often made the news and required extended communication blackouts at home in order to maintain operational secrecy. By this point in the war, we had all been to memorial services for fallen friends and comrades.

If there is one thing the military does right, it's helping people face their own mortality. As part of the predeployment preparation, we had updated our wills, signed powers of attorney, and made a list of which sentimental items of Drew's would go to each child should he not make it home. Of course, posing for the "official death photo," the portrait that could be enlarged to poster size should it be needed for placement next to a casket, was always the most sobering task on that checklist.

As a community of military wives, we lived with the shadow of death and the fear of the unknown every day. It followed us everywhere we went and screamed at us every time we turned on the news. There was an unspoken rule not to bring it up, as if talking about death somehow made it more likely. For me at least, thinking about Drew's possible demise made my fear feel more tangible, so I happily joined the silent movement to avoid the mention of anything morbid.

It was in this context that I had one of the most remarkable conversations of my life. I was enjoying coffee with my friend Lisa on her front porch one bright, sunny day when she turned to me and said, "I've been thinking a lot about what would happen if our husbands were killed."

Immediately, I sat up straighter, shocked that she had just stepped into taboo territory.

"It's not like we would ever want that to happen, or that life would be easy, or that we and our kids wouldn't need counseling or be depressed. But I have determined that if that were to happen, we would be okay. Life would go on, and eventually we'd be all right."

I sat there stunned at her bold revelation. It was as if instead of willfully ignoring the fear of her husband's death like the rest of us, she had turned and stared it straight in the eye. Our husbands' deaths were, at the time, by far the most concrete and gigantic fear in our lives. But as her words slowly sank in, I had to agree. And as we sat there and began to talk about how we would cope, who would come alongside us, and how God was our families' ultimate provider, I felt hope and light begin to dissipate the shadow of our fear. It was the most phenomenal conversation I had ever been a part of. From that moment on, I began to understand this fundamental truth: While we are in the midst of our unique, difficult circumstances, whether combat deployments, illness, financial troubles, loneliness, addiction, relationship struggles, or even rocket launches, God gives each of us the ability to choose the path of either hope or fear. Whether we like it or not, we will live our lives dictated by one or the other, and if we don't make an active decision to choose hope, our default will always be fear.

Fear is reactionary and defensive, and it leads to an eventual downward spiral into despair. Fear tells our hearts that scary, outside forces have dominion over our lives, so we'd better grasp and grapple for whatever scraps of control we can reach. Fear tells us that if the worst thing happens, our lives will no longer be worth living or that everything good in our lives as we know it will be over.

The alternative—hope—isn't blind optimism or denial of reality. Like fear, hope says that our lives are not our own, but unlike fear, hope speaks the truth that a force much greater than current events or our own abilities is in control, and we can rest in that divine power to sustain us. Hope enables us to live confidently and with peace, no matter what happens, because we trust in a God who is with us in both the best and worst of times. In those dark deployment days, sitting through funeral after funeral, I felt God's hope speaking to me, telling me that even if the worst happened and Drew did not come home, life might be different, but it would still be worth living and full of good things. Even so, each day, I had to make a choice. Which path would I travel: fear or hope?

✳   ✳   ✳

3 . . . 2 . . . 1 . . . The engines ignite in a massive explosion and slowly lift the rocket off the ground. We feel it before we hear it. Sonic rumblings travel through the hard ground, and the vibrations course through our feet. The wave of the massive engine roar reaches us, rolling up through our bodies, vibrating in our chests. The fiery blast blinds us as the rocket rises higher and higher into the night sky. The sound is so loud my daughter attempts to press her ear into her shoulder since both hands are tightly held. The light is so bright, it's like looking directly at the sun, and my brain tells me to look away. But I want to see every second of it. Drew is *in there*. So whether the rocket continues to rise off the ground in a glorious arc of fire or suddenly explodes in a massive plume of smoke, I'm watching. Spots appear in my peripheral vision as my eyes attempt to adjust. I allow myself a few gulping sobs, and that small emotional release helps me stay calm. Down at the other, far end of the field, I can hear the cheers and celebration from the space tourists. This is exactly what they've come to see. It's magnificent and awe-inspiring and worth every penny! It's a bucket-list event, and for them, the party has just begun. Back on our side of the field, a heavy silence engulfs us. There are no high fives or fist pumps. We know the crew intimately and understand that we're not out of the woods yet. It feels like a holy moment, standing silently in the dark, surrounded by people watching the rocket travel farther and farther away until it's just a dot of light in the sky, like a distant star.

NASA is tracking the rocket's progress and provides updates each time it successfully passes another risk point. "First stage is complete," my escort tells me at the two-minute mark, meaning that the four external boosters have been successfully jettisoned. We can breathe a little easier now, remembering that a malfunction with the booster separation triggered a ballistic launch abort of a Soyuz carrying NASA astronaut Nick Hague, our good friend, less than a year earlier.

About nine minutes after launch, the next round of messages comes rolling in. "Second stage is complete," my escort tells me with a smile. "Drew's in space."

Stage two is when the core stage separation occurs, and the main body of the rocket drops behind, leaving just the Soyuz capsule containing the crew, now in orbit around the Earth. They've crossed the Kármán line, the altitude—100 km above sea level—that defines where "space" begins. As a group, we collectively exhale. The worst is over! I turn and see my in-laws hugging each other and Drew's brothers. Our guests are smiling and breathlessly chatting with one another in a way that only people who have experienced something monumental together can.

"Can you believe how loud it was? My ears hurt!"

"I didn't realize we'd feel it so much! The ground was moving!"

"That was incredible! Look at this picture!"

"I can't believe how emotional it made me!"

As they banter, they look to me: Is it okay to approach and offer me a hug yet? My friend Lisa, the same Army deployment friend from years ago, steps forward, and we embrace with a wordless sense of relief and joy.

Now that all the flammable fuel rocket components have been jettisoned, Drew's small capsule flying through space at over 17,000 miles per hour feels safe by comparison. More family and friends offer hugs, congratulations, and their thoughts about the launch. Everyone is teary-eyed as they describe how they felt knowing Drew—their son, brother, or friend—was on the rocket they just witnessed break the bonds of gravity.

"Thank you so much for inviting us to be here."

"This was so much more than I could have imagined."

"Look at this video I took of you and the kids backlit by the rocket blast! What an experience!"

The reporters are excitedly describing the launch to their viewers in a cacophony of foreign languages. My brain is trying to process it all, and I still feel as if I'm on a movie set; it just doesn't seem completely real. *How can this be true? Is Drew literally in space?*

We work our way back to the waiting vans and pile inside. It's been less than an hour since we first arrived at the launch viewing area, but it feels far longer. The forty-five-minute drive back to our hotel seems to take forever as the adrenaline starts to wear off and emotional exhaustion sets in. By the time we pull up in front of our hotel, I'm done. Just before the kids and I head up to our rooms, my escort asks if I want to watch the docking in four hours. Docking, when the Soyuz capsule rendezvouses with and physically attaches to the space station, though obviously important, can be boring to watch. You can see the spacecraft getting closer and closer to the station, but you don't see any camera views from inside the capsule, and all the dialogue is technical and in Russian. I choose to try to sleep instead. Hatch opening, when we see the newly arrived crew enter the space station for the first time, will be the more significant event of the day and only a couple of hours after docking. I know we will need at least a little sleep in order to be at our best for that important milestone.

The kids fall asleep quickly. I try to rest too, but my head is spinning. It's the first time all day I've been away from cameras and curious glances. Memories from the day flash across my mind, but they skitter off like fireflies before I can grab one and examine it more closely. I can hear some guests and tourists loudly celebrating in the hotel bar down the hall. Their jubilant songs and euphoric chants are a soundtrack to the tumbling jumble of thoughts and feelings within me. I lie in the dark, thinking about Drew orbiting the Earth, floating in his tiny capsule, a vehicle with about the same internal volume as my minivan. It seems impossible. It's like trying to ponder infinity, a concept just out of reach for my finite brain.

Drew is gone, literally off this planet for nine long months. In many ways, I am now alone on this Earth. I eventually drift off, thinking about Drew floating in zero gravity and wondering what unknown craziness is going to come next.

✳ ✳ ✳

My cell phone alarm jolts me awake. I have a hard time rousing the kids, and they're grumpy. I don't feel so cheerful myself. I take the time to do my hair and makeup because I know we will be on camera again. The knot in my stomach has been replaced with the low-level nausea that comes with sleep deprivation. We'll be watching the hatch opening from inside an old theater on the other side of Baikonur, so our group of family and guests meet in the lobby to board the vans once again. I'm quick to pawn my kids off on relatives who are far more tolerant of their complaining than I am at this time of the morning.

After a short drive, the vehicles pull up outside the theater. Again, it's like something out of a movie set. Soviet-built, the stark architecture in this remote location makes it seem as if we are reporting for secret training, not a televised event. The street outside is deserted, but the lobby is bustling with activity. Friendly local women are serving juice, champagne, fruit, and cookies to whoever can stomach them at this early hour. As much as I want to let loose with a swig of bubbly, my stomach warns that a celebratory drink would probably not be a good idea. I settle for some juice instead.

"Mom, I don't feel so good." My oldest daughter, Amelia, appears at my side looking pale and unsteady. "I think I might throw up."

She has the same lack-of-sleep stomachache I do. The high temperatures, even at this early morning hour, and the building's lack of air-conditioning aren't helping.

I scan the room for a quiet corner where I can park her for a few minutes before heading inside the auditorium.

"Sit here," I tell her. "Take deep breaths and drink some of this juice. And if you think you're going to be sick, use this." I pull over a trash can. Having watched the hatch openings of several of our astronaut friends, I know there is a NASA TV camera crew inside the auditorium, and we don't need live coverage of my daughter vomiting for the world to see.

A general murmur rolls through the crowded lobby, and my escort says it's time to go inside. The old theater has two levels: the main floor and a slightly elevated balcony toward the back. The crew families are directed to sit in the balcony's front row so we have an unobstructed view of the large movie screen set up on the stage. The stagnant air is sweltering, and mercifully someone pulls an old pedestal fan to the side of the balcony and turns it on. It slowly oscillates back and forth but doesn't do much to help cool the air in this big space. My kids sit oldest to youngest next to me, and we can see our family and friends sitting below us. As we wait, sweat running down the back of our necks and legs, a few confused bats swoop across the room, brushing their wings against the peeling paint on the ceiling. I'm struggling to keep a smile on my face as I watch my kids wiggle and poke each other, trying to get comfortable in the old seats. To our left, the NASA TV crew has set up their camera and are panning the room, occasionally swiveling toward us in the front row. The heat, the bats, the kids, the nausea, the waiting—it's too much.

With no warning, the screen flickers on and the live coverage begins. In front of us is a live video feed from one of the Russian modules inside the space station. In the middle of the screen, we see a short hallway, like a tube, receding back a few feet before dead-ending on the closed hatch, which reminds me of something I'd see on a submarine. The astronauts already on the space station, our friends Nick Hague and Christina Koch, occasionally bob into the shot as they wait. The Russian commander hovers by the entrance to the hatch hallway. Nick and Christina move in closer, looking as anxious to see the new crew emerge as we are. There is no sound with the video feed, so we try to guess what they are saying. It's clear they're all waiting on the green light from Russian mission control to open the hatch. Suddenly, there is a flurry of activity and the hatch starts to move. It reminds me of watching an eclipse; it seems to start slowly and then picks up speed. As the hatch swings down into the capsule, the station's Russian commander and his counterpart in the Soyuz work together to wrestle the cumbersome metal door into place.

Aleksandr, the Soyuz commander, is first out. A grandfather and veteran of two spaceflights, his previous experience is obvious. He floats into the module confidently, hugging the crew and effortlessly moving to the side to make room.

We're not sure who will be next to emerge, and we hold our breath as we wait. It's Drew! I watch as my husband pulls himself into the module with his arms, his legs floating stiffly behind him. He happily, albeit clumsily, hugs his classmate Christina, her curly hair bouncing with each excited squeeze. Drew pivots off Christina to grab Nick, one of his best friends and the person I know he is most excited to see. They embrace in what feels like the world's longest recorded man-hug. (Watching the coverage again later, we timed the hug at a remarkable ten full seconds.) They both look elated. I'm stunned. Is this for real? How can the man I was reminding to take out the trash just last month be *in space*? He is *floating*! He is smiling! This is crazy.

We watch the group awkwardly fumble and bump into each other as they arrange themselves in the module. The newly doubled crew spreads out in two rows of three, new arrivals in the front, old crew in the back. The three new arrivals—Drew, Luca Parmitano of Italy, and Aleksandr Skvortsov from Russia—put on headsets that allow them to communicate with the ground. They can't see us, but they can hear us. Now it's our turn to perform for the cameras.

Weeks earlier, we'd been prepped about this part of the hatch opening ceremony. One by one, each family will be handed a phone connected to mission control, allowing us to talk with the crew. Each person will be given an opportunity to speak with their astronaut, and the audio is connected to the live video feed that NASA TV is recording, so it will all be streamed for the world to see and hear.

You'd better believe I wasn't going to hand my eight-year-old a microphone to the world without a little preparation. Earlier in the week, I grabbed an envelope from my hotel room and told each kid to write down just one sentence to say to their father when the phone was handed to them. I practiced with the younger two until they could say their sentences clearly and without giggles or weird inflections. This exercise seemed silly and pointless to them at the time, and I had to bribe them with candy to repeat it over and over. Now, as the phone is brought to our section, I can see in their eyes that they wish they had practiced a little more.

Aleksandr's wife goes first, speaking Russian, but the sentiment is clear: "The launch was great; I love you." Next comes Luca's American wife and his two daughters, speaking English. They ask how he felt during the ride up and wish him good luck. Then it's our turn. The NASA TV camera swings in our direction as the phone is passed to my youngest. I hand her the envelope with her words written on the back, and she reads them out loud into the phone receiver: "Daddy, I love you forever and always."

There is a short delay as the audio signal routes through Moscow's mission control and shoots into outer space. Her eyes light up when we hear her words echoing into the astronaut headsets, and Drew responds with a voice full of emotion. "I love you too. I love you very much. Keep thinking about us and praying for us."

As the phone moves down the row, the children each say their prepared lines, and Drew responds, saying how much he loves them and misses them already. Drew's eyes are misty, and his face is tight. His crewmate Christina pats him on the back, recognizing his strain. As the phone is handed to me, I look down, momentarily thrown by the fact that the receiver looks like an old cordless model we owned a decade ago. Somehow I had expected something more high-tech. I glance at my prepared sentence and wish I had thought of something more profound.

"Drew, the launch was surreal. We are so proud of you. This will be such an amazing adventure. We love you."

"I love you guys so much," Drew responds. "It was an incredible ride. It is surreal to be here." He wipes his eyes and pumps his fist toward the camera.

At that moment, I am thinking only of his outer space adventure— Drew floating through the station, performing spacewalks, and doing the seemingly impossible while orbiting the planet. As I think about what's next, I know this journey did not begin when the rocket launched, just as it will not end when it lands. This journey began years, if not decades ago, when Drew and I together chose this life, one full of excitement and fun and adventure, but also risk and heartbreak and danger.

And I can see now that the first big reason we've been able to thrive and not just survive is that no matter what comes up in life, we actively choose hope. Not a hope based on wishes and dreams, rainbows and unicorns, blissful happy endings, or even our own abilities. It's the kind of hope we are offered each day, with God's strength, to look our fears and uncertainties straight in the eye and continue to move forward, no matter what happens, because he is with us and will enable us to do what must be done. It's the kind of hope we have to choose anew each morning, the type of gutsy hope we hear in Esther's voice when she says, "If I perish, I perish."

So as the video feed ends and I think of my husband orbiting far above the Earth in his new home for the next nine months, I know I have only one choice: I choose hope.

CHAPTER 2

SPACEWALKS, BOLOGNA, AND BLIND DATES

FIND YOUR PEOPLE

I was a plucky, overconfident eighteen-year-old when I met Drew, a fellow cadet at West Point. He was two years ahead of me, and we both fully embraced the experience we'd been told would be the hardest four years of our lives. Unlike Drew, I'd ended up at West Point through a series of happy accidents. I was a well-rounded student and strong athlete at my Massachusetts high school. I was also in the band and involved with my church's youth group, going on mission trips and bonding with our youth leader. Despite my many interests, I had no passion for any one subject or career path that might steer my future in a particular direction.

"Where do you want to go to college?" a teacher asked me at the start of my junior year. I'm sure she expected me to rattle off the usual list of competitive colleges my classmates were considering, such as UMass, Boston College, Harvard, or MIT, all of which were less than an hour away.

"Um, I haven't really narrowed it down yet," I equivocated. The reality was, I hadn't thought much about anything past next week's math test.

"Perhaps you should go visit the guidance counselors' office," she suggested. "They could really help you."

"Yeah, great idea," I said as I slowly drifted away, wanting to get to the lunchroom where my friends were waiting.

A week later I wandered through the counseling center where rows upon rows of colorful college brochures lined the room. As I walked along the wall, my finger dragging across the edge of the metal racks, nothing jumped out at me. But when I reached the corner of the room, I noticed a small section labeled "Military" hidden behind a chair. A single pamphlet, one of only three options in that section, caught my eye. It was a brochure for the US Air Force Band, and as a passable French horn player, the idea of getting paid to play music was intriguing. I stuffed the pamphlet into the back pocket of my faded jeans and headed to class.

That night, I pulled out the pamphlet and turned on the family computer, the screeching tones of dial-up internet filling the living room. With just a little research, I realized I was not a good enough, or dedicated enough, musician to join the Air Force Band. But in my searching, I stumbled across the website for the United States Military Academy at West Point, New York, most commonly referred to as simply West Point. Immediately, my interest was piqued. It was far enough away from home to offer me some distance, but not too far for my parents to visit.

West Point was looking for smart, athletic leaders of character. Check, check, and check. My family had minimal experience with the military, but the price tag—free!—was appealing. Since I had no plans whatsoever for next week, let alone for a career, maybe the

Army could help me figure that out. I typed in my name and mailing address and requested more information.

A month later, I scheduled an appointment with my guidance counselor. The West Point materials had arrived, and I loved everything I'd read so far. I'd never actually met this counselor before, and I knew as little about her as she did about me. But all the same, I wanted her to see the materials and agree that West Point was a perfect fit for me.

"I think West Point sounds really great," I told her with an expectant look as I handed over the glossy folder about the application process.

She looked down at the packet, then back up at me. "The Army?" she said with disbelief. "You do know that's what this is, right? Kids from this school, with your grades, with your test scores, with your extracurriculars, don't just *join the Army*. No one from here does that."

Well, I thought. *That's all I need to know. I'm going to West Point.*

The application process to all military academies is purposely long and arduous to weed out those who are applying only to appease their parents or for any reason other than a deep personal desire. It includes medical and dental exams, essay writing, a physical fitness test, and interviews. As you are completing those requirements, you also have to apply for a congressional nomination, which is a completely different and equally challenging process. I saw it all as a personal challenge and barreled through it, passing each test and securing every needed recommendation by charming the alumni interviewers with my big smile and open confidence. By Christmas break of my senior year, I had my offer of admission from West Point. My parents were slightly confused and nervous about my choice, but I accepted immediately—after all, it was the only school I'd applied to.

A few years earlier, down in Delaware, a boy I'd never met had completed the same application, but his impetus for applying had been quite different. The firstborn son of an Air Force colonel, Drew Morgan always knew he wanted to be a military officer. An early visit to West Point had cemented the place in his mind as his destiny, but he figured he'd apply to the Air Force Academy too, just in case. A calm, methodical thinker, he carefully worked through each stage of the application process, acing every test, double-checking every box, humbly shaking every hand, each day one step closer to the future he envisioned for himself. He would be a career Army officer, and attending West Point was the natural first step.

By spring 1997, we'd been living on the same small campus for almost a full year, our paths surely crossing time and time again but never meeting. Drew was a junior, a "cow," and already a rising leader in his class. As a freshman "plebe," I was busy delivering laundry bundles to upperclassmen, playing sports, and keeping up with my studies, which required a level of academic rigor I had never experienced in high school. So while I had attended church regularly growing up, finding time to plug into a faith community while at West Point was easier said than done. The only day of the week when I had even a remote chance to sleep past 6 a.m. was Sunday, and I loved to sleep. Attending Sunday morning services was never going to happen. As an alternative, several faith-based clubs met during the week. My friend Sarah and I began attending Officers' Christian Fellowship, which met on Tuesday nights. We liked the sense of community there, as well as meeting fun and interesting cadets from all four classes. This was one of the few places where rank, a big deal for a plebe at the bottom of the ladder, was put aside.

In the spring, Sarah and I signed up to go on the Easter retreat, a three-day trip to a camp in the mountains. We couldn't wait to get away from the stress of barracks life, and more important to us, wear civilian clothes for a few days. On Saturday morning of the retreat,

Sarah and I headed to the camp chapel for the morning program. I took little notice of the guy sitting at the other end of the pew. As the pastor wrapped up his message, he challenged us to partner with someone to talk about what we'd learned. I turned to Sarah, only to find her already in conversation with the girl to her right. When I turned to my left, I was surprised to discover that the boy at the end of the pew had already scooted next to me.

"Hi," he said. "I'm Drew."

"Oh, hi," I said, still surprised whenever an upperclassman used their first rather than their last name, something that had only recently been allowed for plebes. "I'm Stacey. I guess we're supposed to discuss the message?"

"Yes, let's talk!" he replied. He told me later he'd chosen his seat hoping we'd have to pair up.

We chatted about ourselves, then we told each other our struggles. We kept talking on the way to lunch. We met up during free time and discussed our families and our friends. We joked while I beat him in a game of Ping-Pong and continued our conversation at dinner. And the next day, when we got on the bus for the long ride back to the academy, we sat together. When I pretended to be tired so I could put my head on his shoulder, he pretended to be tired too, so he could rest his head on top of mine.

As we got to know each other better, the differences in our approach to academy life—and life in general—became clear. We both liked structure and rules, but for different reasons. Drew liked knowing where the line was so he could stay far away from it. I liked knowing where the line was so I could dance along the edge of it. For example, regulation clearly stated that cadets were allowed only three personal knickknacks on their shelves. Just to be safe, Drew had none. I, in contrast, read the regulation and realized no rules were given about our computer monitors, still a relatively new addition to the cadet desk. By the end of the first semester, the frame of my computer screen was covered in pictures and gaudy decorations, while my three allowed knickknacks were lined up neatly on the shelf above my desk.

Drew enjoyed the simplicity and harshness of military life. He wore only issued clothes, had his hair cut extra short, and moved briskly between academic classes and practice sessions with the free-fall parachute team. When practice ended, he went directly to dinner and then headed back to his room to study for the rest of the night. He worked better under stress, so he put it on himself and excelled in a system that valued his hard work, dedication, and commitment to service. He was, in many ways, the ideal cadet. He wanted to go to medical school after graduation and knew that he needed to do well at West Point to do so.

Whereas Drew naturally blended in, I embraced the fact that I stood out. Only 10 percent of the cadet corps were women at the time, so it wasn't hard to do. I openly debated with male classmates about women attending the Citadel, which had opened to females just a year earlier. I socialized whenever I could, hanging out in other people's rooms at night and attending dances on weekends.

I flexed the edges of my freedoms and did everything I could to make myself more comfortable. Like most female cadets, I began to grow out my hair as soon as I was permitted to do so. I wore makeup and earrings with every authorized uniform. I kept my toenails brightly painted, and I bought expensive shampoo and flowery lotion to rub on my skin every day. Under my heavily starched uniform, I wore pink underwear. The first half of the plebe year, when we weren't yet allowed to listen to music in our rooms, I stumbled upon the record collection in the library and from that day on, spent several nights a week secretly locked in one of the small audio rooms listening to whatever music was available while I studied. I didn't mind pushing against the system because I knew that as long as I didn't cross the line, the academy would take me where I needed to go. Where that was exactly—who knew? But I'd do my best to enjoy the ride.

If Drew lived in the black-and-white of the academy system, I was most comfortable in the gray between. And yet when we started spending more time together, integrating our approaches added a new dimension to our lives in a way neither of us could have anticipated.

The first time I visited Drew's room and sat down at his desk, I immediately noticed the lack of personal items on his shelf. "Why don't you have some pictures of your family or something?" I asked him. "Your side of the room looks like the example room in the West Point Museum."

"It does?" he asked. "I guess I never really thought about it."

I opened his desk drawer. Everything was lined up where it should be. I pulled out his box of colored pencils, the same ones I had. Standard issue.

"We're going to need to change that," I said, as I started moving things around.

"Uh, okay," he said, shifting a little uncomfortably in his seat.

When I got up to head back to my barracks on the other side of campus, I watched Drew sit back down at his desk and stare in disbelief at his calendar. There, in a riot of colors and squiggles, was my name, doodled in two-inch-high letters across the bottom of the page. A couple of weeks later, when the month was over and it was time to flip the calendar page, he cut out my name and propped it against his computer screen. He now had his one and only knickknack.

Over the next year, we took walks and went to the movies. I cheered him on as he parachuted into Michie Stadium at the start of every football game. He cheered me on from the sidelines of my lacrosse games. In quiet moments when we sat together on a rock overlooking the Hudson River, he asked me questions I'd never considered before: What did I want to do after graduation? What kind of job did I want? Where did I want to live? Did I want to have any pets? Get married? Have a family?

I admitted that I hadn't really thought much about those things before I met him. Then one day I added, "But I know whatever I do, I want to do it all with you."

✳ ✳ ✳

August 21, 2019
Friendswood, Texas

I groan as I roll out of bed, the alarm from my smart speaker gradually getting louder and louder until I mumble, "Alexa, stop!" Bleary-eyed, I stumble into the bathroom. When my feet hit the cold tile, I wake up just enough to remember that this is not a regular day. I squint into my phone screen and open YouTube. It's just after 6 a.m., which means it's 11 a.m. on the space station, and the crew has been hard at work for hours. Adjusting my glasses, I pull up the NASA Live channel. My heart beats a little faster when the real-time video from inside the space station flicks on. I see that Drew and his crewmate Nick are already wearing their cooling garments, the long-johns-looking space underwear covered in thin rubber tubes that regulate body temperature inside the cumbersome space suit.

Today is Drew's first spacewalk. This event is a huge deal to every astronaut, made all the more special for Drew because he's going outside with one of his best friends, Nick. I want to watch as much of the live coverage as possible, so I take one more glance at the screen before scurrying into the closet to grab my clothes. I'm rushing so

I don't miss a minute, even though I know it will take Drew a little more time and a lot more effort to put on all the different components of his space suit, technically known as an extravehicular mobility unit (EMU).

By the time I dash into the living room and pull up the NASA coverage on our television, Drew and Nick already have the pants to their space suits on and are squeezing their way into the upper torso of the suit. Their arms are extended over their heads like toddlers putting on bulky sweaters. I crank up the volume so the kids can hear the NASA commentary as they slowly make their way downstairs. It may be a big day for Drew, but the kids are far more concerned about what's for breakfast than the momentous event in their father's life playing out on the TV in front of them.

"Hurry up!" I yell. "Daddy goes out the hatch at 7:15. I want you all here on the couch, shoes on, bags packed, ready to go before that so you can watch!"

If everything stays on schedule, everyone should be able to see the start of the spacewalk and still get to school on time. The kids will have seven minutes to watch in amazement and appreciate that they have the coolest dad in the universe before the younger kids have to run outside at 7:22 to catch the bus. Then about ten minutes later, the older kids will need to leave.

The kids grumble and seem to shift into a slower gear, if that's even possible. Daniel blinks slowly at me. "We're out of Life cereal."

I watch the TV out of the corner of my eye while throwing silverware in the dishwasher, grabbing lunches out of the fridge, and pulling hair into ponytails. Drew and Nick finish suiting up, and their crewmates stuff them into the air lock, the small module designed for transferring people and cargo in and out of the station. It has two airtight doors, one leading into the ISS and the other out into space.

Once the astronauts are jammed inside, the doors are sealed and the chamber is slowly depressurized to match the vacuum outside Earth's atmosphere. Only then can Drew and Nick open the external hatch and float out into space.

With a little more yelling and a lot more complaining, all four kids get to the couch, teeth brushed, shoes on, by 7:14. The minutes tick by, and the school bus arrival time creeps closer as we wait for the big moment. The kids are as anxious as I am; they don't want to miss the bus almost as much as I don't want them to miss this moment. At 7:22, the hatch is still closed, and the live video feed is showing only extreme close-up shots of the air lock walls that Drew's and Nick's helmet cameras are wedged against.

"Stay here and keep watching," I tell the older two. "I've got to put your sisters on the bus."

I grab my phone and pull up the coverage on the YouTube app again. As we jog to the bus stop, I try to keep the screen in front of the girls' faces. Still no movement from the air lock as the school bus turns the corner and squeals to a stop in front of us. After I give the girls quick goodbye kisses, they skip to the steps and climb inside the waiting bus.

Shoot!

They've missed their dad's big moment and will have to watch the recording when they get home later that afternoon. I let out a frustrated huff and dash back to the house.

As I dart into the living room and focus my attention on the TV, I see a set of puffy legs sticking straight up out of the hatch, the white pants a stark contrast with the deep black of space. In the minute it took me to get back inside the house, Nick has already egressed (the fancy space word for "exited") the space station and is waiting patiently as Drew emerges, feet first, into the void of space. I look around the room, but the older kids are nowhere to be found.

"Where are you?" I holler. "Your father is coming out of the hatch into flipping space!"

Alone, I plunk down on the couch, my irritation taking some of the shine off what I'm seeing on the TV screen. Drew fully backs himself out and holds on to the thin railing that wraps around the opening to the air lock. I know it's him, but the bulky, pressurized suit makes his movements stiff, slow, and slightly robotic. The video coverage alternates between wide shots of Drew and Nick moving on the outside of the station, streamed from mounted external cameras, and helmet camera views, where I can see Drew's hands working in front of him as if we are looking through his eyes. He's clipping and unclipping himself to different parts of the station as he and Nick get their bearings and make their way toward the work site.

I've known Drew for so long, I know exactly what's going on in his head right now. He's got a single thought on a repeat loop: *Don't screw up. Don't screw up. Don't screw up.*

He won't screw up, of that I can be sure. Together, he and Nick are methodical, skilled, and well-practiced. Drew told me about the work they'd be doing today—uncoiling and attaching what seems like miles of new electrical cords to the outside of the station. Sitting on my own couch, coffee mug in hand, I recognize that now-familiar disconnected feeling of watching Drew float in the vacuum of space in his own personal spaceship. Like the launch, it seems too fantastic, too easy to watch, to be true. The older kids wander back in the room, gazing at the television for a few lingering moments before kissing me goodbye and heading out to school.

"See you later," Amelia says.

"Can we have pizza for dinner tonight?" Daniel asks.

I'm amazed by their ability to take these unparalleled life events in stride. Then again, I realize being an astronaut's kid puts each of them in a strange position. As an Army officer and now an astronaut, Drew was often gone for months at a time so his absence was felt in our kids' lives, but was not shocking or overly disruptive to them. Even though we want them to appreciate the incredible privilege it is to be a part of space exploration, we don't want who they are, how they see themselves, or the entirety of their childhoods to be defined by their father's profession. And honestly, they know at least a dozen other kids of astronauts and are close friends with many of them. As a result, these mind-bending and history-making events do not feel unique to them. Another spacewalk? What's the big deal? Their friend's dad did one just a month ago and another friend's mom will do one soon. I like to think that in twenty years they'll look back and marvel at the unbelievable events they were a part of. But for now, it's just another Wednesday.

As the front door slams behind them, I remember a conversation I had two years earlier with Amy Bean, daughter of Apollo astronaut Alan Bean, the fourth man to walk on the moon. She told me that on the day her dad walked on the moon for the first time, her mom woke her up to watch the coverage on television. After it was over, Amy took a short nap and then her mom sent her to school. After all, what would have been the point of her hanging around the house all day? We laughed together when she told that story because it so perfectly reflected the experience of astronaut families: a series of amazing, surreal events, all wrapped up in the everyday, mundane tasks of life. Fifty years later, it seems my kids are simply following in Amy's footsteps.

I take one last sip of coffee before grabbing my purse and jumping in the car. I have no time to lose if I'm going to make it to mission control by 8 a.m. as planned. I keep my phone app open so I can listen to the spacewalk coverage while I drive the twenty minutes to

Johnson Space Center, NASA's center for human spaceflight. I can hear the clipped conversation between the astronauts and the ground, but without the visual cues, it's impossible to understand.

"Copy Drew, you are go to translate up the CETA spur, and you are headed to the starboard CETA cart. We'll call your WIF five for the APFR once you get there. Just a reminder, do not fairlead your tether as you translate."[5]

"Copy." Drew's voice sounds like Darth Vader's and is almost unrecognizable. I have no idea what they're talking about.

Once at the Johnson Space Center gate, I show my badge and find my parking spot outside Building 30. The plain, windowless exterior of the Christopher C. Kraft Jr. Mission Control Center conceals a hive of technology and communications equipment capable of connecting people both around—and off—the planet. I jog into the lobby where my chaperone, a NASA employee, waits. She swipes her badge across the access panel that unlocks the thick metal doors, and we hustle upstairs to the flight control viewing area.

On spacewalk days, this room is reserved for family and invited guests only. When I walk in, the only person sitting in one of the seventy auditorium-style seats is my family escort, the same astronaut who supported me at the launch just one month earlier. He smiles and hands me a cup of coffee as I drop my purse and settle in next to him.

In front of us, behind thick glass windows, are the two dozen mission control consoles that monitor every aspect of the International Space Station. For a spacewalk, technically known as an extravehicular activity (EVA), the consoles are manned by highly trained NASA engineers. I watch as each system expert stares at his or her bank of computer monitors, poised to react if there's an issue. On the front wall of the room are three huge screens displaying every available camera angle for the EVA and columns upon columns of data, none of which mean anything to me. On the middle screen I see Drew and Nick outside of the station, their hands working methodically on the tasks in front of them. As my escort leans over and quietly updates me on the long list of procedure steps they need to complete within the seven-hour spacewalk window, I hear a babble of voices in the hallway. Catie Hague, Nick's wife and my good friend, appears in the doorway. Her phone is tucked under her arm, and she carries a coffee in one hand and a bowl of homemade salsa and a bag of chips in the other. Trailing behind her is Nick's mom, visiting from out of town, with three more food containers containing cookies and other treats piled in her arms. The sudden influx of people and snacks makes it feel more like we're hosting a Super Bowl party than overseeing the somber vigil this experience could easily become.

"Hey, everyone! Can you believe I just spilled salsa all over my shirt! I knew this bowl was going to leak. Are there any napkins in here? Look at my shirt! I have to wear this all day. Mom, put all that food on the back table! Are there any paper towels back there? What'd I miss? Where are they in the procedure? Are they behind or ahead?"

Catie's firecracker personality fills the room as she peppers our escort with questions and drops the bowl of salsa and bag of chips on the back table. She heads toward the row of seats where I'm sitting, throwing her phone on a chair and immediately asking how the spacewalk has unfolded so far.

"Have they finished with the first task yet?" she asks me.

"Yes, they're already on to the second. They're working really well together."

"What was that deal with Drew's glove I heard him talking about?"

"I don't know, something about a flap of the rubber coming up

42

on one of the fingers? No one has said anything to me about it, so I guess they're not too concerned."

"Hmm," she says. "We'll see what the flight director says about it."

Only four weeks into Drew's nine-month mission, I am still very much the rookie, taking my cues whenever I can from experienced "flown" spouses like Catie. Nick has already been on board for over five months, and this is his third spacewalk, so Catie's a pro. Her relaxed posture while she chats with the flight director and the NASA people who float in and out of the room, combined with her subtle but vigilant monitoring of the giant screens, gives me a sense of comfort. Over the past several years, Catie and I have bonded through our shared NASA family experience. But more recently, she has become my guide and confidant, a close friend I can count on to keep the secret fears and frustrations about the mission I pour out to her during our weekly margarita sessions.

She knows how this day is supposed to go and what the space-to-ground chatter should sound like. She can tell if things are going well by the body language of the experts below us on the floor of mission control. If something goes sideways, she'll pick up on it right away, so if she's relaxed, I'm relaxed.

"Everything is going really well," she says to me. "We've got five more hours of this. Let's eat some cookies."

A short time later, my friend and invited guest, Allison, arrives. She has never been at mission control before, so her excitement and curiosity are contagious. Catie and I happily answer all her questions and laugh at her insightful, outsider-looking-in commentary about the spacewalk experience.

"What's that number up there on the screen mean?" Allison asks.

"That's how many hours and minutes they've been outside."

"Which video feed is Drew's and which is Nick's?"

"Drew's on the right, Nick is on the left."

"Do you think their arms are tired?"

"Drew told me that it's usually their hands that feel the worst the next day."

"Whoever is talking to them on the radio," notes Allison, "has a supersoothing voice."

"That's Mike Barratt, another astronaut. He's the ground IV,[6] the only person who talks to the crew during an EVA."

"I bet they are so hungry when this is all over."

"Yes, and they really have to go to the bathroom."

When I woke up this morning, I had no idea what to expect from this unusual day. Other spouses of astronauts who'd gone on spacewalks offered me a range of descriptions for how they felt while watching the event—from calling it the most stressful seven hours of their lives to the most boring half day they could remember. When everything goes as planned, spacewalks are long, tedious events to watch with only quick, glorious glimpses of the bright blue Earth sprinkled across five to seven hours of close-up hand coverage from the helmet cameras. Because astronauts make it look so easy and negative outcomes are so rare, it is easy to forget how inherently dangerous it is to be outside the ISS. A torn glove, a foggy helmet, a leaking valve, a suit malfunction, a micro-meteor strike, or a mistake in the procedure—I know there are countless ways Drew's EVA could be ruined and his life put at risk. Yet sitting in this seat at mission control, surrounded by friends and allies—my people—I feel connected to community, supported and confident. Today I can't imagine navigating this bizarre space expedition journey without trusted friends around me, but as I think back to our move to Houston, I know that could easily have happened.

* * *

August 2013

Before we moved to Houston, I'd never felt humidity like that of a coastal Texas summer. It was the climate equivalent of a hot, steamy washcloth thrown on my face every time I stepped outside. The previous month had been a whirlwind of handling logistics so we could leave the DC area and settle the family near Johnson Space Center before Drew's first day of training.

Prior to Drew being selected by NASA that June, our family had been eagerly anticipating an upcoming move to Stuttgart, Germany, where the Army planned to station Drew next. Packers who specialized in international household shipments were due to arrive in two weeks, and I was mentally prepared for several delightful years of traipsing through Europe and learning conversational German. But within days of Drew's invitation to join NASA's twenty-first class of astronauts, all the planning and paperwork for Germany had to be unraveled, then resubmitted, rescheduled, and mentally readjusted for Texas.

Drew remained an active-duty Army officer, but he was now assigned to NASA. After out-processing from our base in northern Virginia, we hurriedly drove across the country, bought a house, enrolled our kids in school, unpacked our boxes, and hung our pictures on the walls. As Drew headed off to his new job and I shifted my focus to smoothing out our new routines, I was too busy to notice how different everything felt from what we were used to. To the casual observer, my life probably looked the same as it always had—I worked around the house, joined a gym, and took my youngest girls to and from preschool while we waited for their older siblings to get home from school. I joined a moms' group, checked out books from the library, shopped at the grocery store, and picked up dry cleaning. I made dinner, watched television, and called my mom to check in. I did everything I'd done at every other place we'd lived, and yet things were not the same. For the first time, the kids were old enough that they missed their old house, old school, and old friends, so their transition was bumpy and full of angst.

The first month of school was particularly difficult. The day before it started, one of the two cats we'd just dragged across the country with us disappeared, probably eaten by a lurking predator. The kids brought home a stream of parent handouts full of acronyms I did not understand and references to online portals I did not know how to access. At every bedtime, at least one child cried over lost friends, lost pets, or their lost way of life. I wanted to cry with them.

We'd always lived in towns accustomed to military families coming and going, where everything is explained in simple language. Neighbors show up on your doorstep holding plates of cookies and index cards with their names and contact info. Your kid is one of dozens of new kids in their class, each of them born in a different state or overseas. Transitions aren't seamless, but the military community encourages you to get settled and plugged in as fast as possible, greasing the skids for that quick adjustment in ways I hadn't fully appreciated before now. In Virginia, and in North Carolina before that, I had close neighbors and friends, strong community ties, and a respected leadership role in MOPS International, a dynamic ministry for moms that I was passionate about. Now I had none of those things.

Meanwhile, Drew's astronaut class was small—only eight people, affectionately known as the "8-Balls"—so they bonded quickly. Within weeks they were bantering like siblings and felt as if they'd known one another for years. I, on the other hand, felt very alone. At the time, only two other 8-Ball spouses lived in town, and while we tried to help each other, it was the blind leading the blind. We were lost and didn't know where to go for help. I was confused to discover that the same activities, routines, and habits I had engaged in when starting other assignments were not leading to new friendships.

Maybe it's just too early, I thought. *These things take time.*

I met my neighbors and tried to build connections.

"I love your accent!" an adorable Southern belle said to me one morning at the bus stop. She'd caught a subtle hint of my Boston upbringing in my voice that slides in only when I say a few select words and phrases. I didn't have the heart to tell her that between the two of us, it wasn't me who had the accent. Upon learning that Drew was an active-duty Army officer who had deployed to Iraq and Afghanistan, she was visibly startled. It was clear she had never met anyone who had been, in her words, "in the war."

"Does he struggle with any PTSD issues?" she asked in hushed tones while we stood on the street outside her house.

"What? No, but that's . . ." I trailed off, seeing the relief on her face and realizing we didn't have the shared vocabulary to talk about my family's wartime experience.

Until that moment, I had taken for granted the fact that in every other place we'd lived, all the families around us had experienced at least one deployment. We didn't have to talk about the burdens of war; they were simply part of our shared community experience. But when we did talk about it, it was without pity, shame, or justification. We didn't have to explain the why, how, or what that so many of my conversations with new acquaintances in Houston required. The thought of wading into that emotional and political minefield was exhausting, so I deflected it whenever possible. I also avoided telling new acquaintances that Drew was an astronaut because as soon as we dropped the "a-bomb," the dynamic of the conversation immediately changed. We wanted people to like us for *us*, not for the attention Drew's job brought to our family.

When months went by and I still had no meaningful friendships, I struggled to understand why. I'd been clinging to the friendships I'd formed in Virginia and North Carolina, but they started to fade away as the circumstances that had tied us together—like living next door, having a kid in the same class, or attending the same moms group—no longer existed. Sure, I'd met plenty of women who were friendly, but none had become my friends. I began to see myself as an outsider, unable to crack into any established friend circles.

Those first few months passed by in a blur of bitterness and resentment. One morning, I snapped at Drew as he was heading out the door.

"Have a nice day at your dream job, while I'm left here alone to take care of everyone and everything else," I fumed.

Drew glanced at me sideways, a quizzical look on his face, then headed out the door. I headed into the laundry room to angrily whip some towels into the clothes dryer.

Later that night, after the kids were asleep in bed, Drew cornered me in the bathroom.

"What's wrong with you?" he asked, looking at me with the same sincere concern I would give a wounded animal. "You are not yourself lately."

"I know what I said was ugly," I admitted. "I'm sorry. I think there is something wrong with me. I feel so angry and so lonely."

"I think you need something I can't give you," he suggested. "I think you need some friends."

He was right. No matter how hard I tried to ignore it, it was undeniable that I had a need that Drew, the kids, my house, shopping, exercising, or chocolate cake couldn't fill. I needed local girlfriends, and I needed them badly.

After one particularly hard morning, I drove to the gym and pulled into the parking lot. As I turned off the car, I sat for a moment, staring out the windshield. I felt completely alone and at the end of my emotional rope. Overwhelmed with loneliness, I began to ugly cry. Huge tears rolled down my face as I pressed my forehead into the top of the steering wheel. Sobbing loudly, I picked up my phone and called Lisa, the friend I could always count on for wise counsel, no matter how dire or complicated things were.

*　*　*

When we moved to North Carolina in 2005, I didn't know Lisa very well. Our husbands had gone to medical school together, but Lisa and I both worked full-time and saw each other only occasionally. But now we were moving to the same military town at the same time, and I was thrilled to know there'd be at least one person I could talk to as we started this new assignment with Army Special Forces. While we were still making our way to the East Coast, baby in the back seat, my phone rang.

"Hey, it's Lisa! I've been in town a couple of weeks now, and I have it all figured out." She told me the name of the best grocery store where coupons weren't required and the local gym that offered a military discount. She told me she had discovered a great moms' morning out program, and since they still had openings, she'd emailed me the paperwork. "Given what I know of your theological bent," Lisa told me, "this is the first church you'll want to try. I've already signed us both up for the local MOPS group; it's the best moms' group around. *And* I've already met a great group of ladies I can't wait to introduce you to. Sound good?"

"Um, okay. Sounds good."

"Great! See you in a few days. Bye!"

There are times when I like doing research, sorting the data, and fully owning my unique choices. This was not one of those times. From day one, I was happy to grab on and ride Lisa's coattails. Lisa was what I call a "seed friend," someone who invites you into their circle and helps plug you in with others. An amazing networker, gifted communicator, and thoughtful confidant, she quickly introduced me to a cohort of women who would become my closest friends. Because we lived in a small, military-heavy community, it was natural for us to be members of the same gym, have kids in the same school, shop in the same stores, and know the same people. Most important, all our husbands were assigned to Special Forces units on the same military base, so we shared a deep understanding of duty, honor, service, and sacrifice.

On paper, the five years we spent in North Carolina should have been some of the hardest of my life. Between combat deployments, long-distance training events, and military schools, Drew was away from home almost three of those five years. We had two more children in that time, bringing our family total to three kids under the age of six. I had no ties or family in the area, and I carried the daily stress of knowing that Drew was participating in dangerous, secretive work that could result in life-threatening injuries or death. Yet those years were some of the richest of my life. Our group of friends bonded over the shared grief of friends killed in action, the shared joy of reunion, and the shared struggles of maintaining a healthy marriage and family in a world driven by a high-tempo deployment cycle. We wives prioritized our friendships, meeting together formally for coffee dates and book studies, and informally at the pool, at the park, or on front porches. The time we spent together, combined with living in the same town and sharing the toll from the high-risk careers of our husbands, was the fuel that kept our friendship engine going strong.

We became what Lisa called "bologna is on sale" friends—friends with whom you "do life" so intimately that you share the most mundane of life's day-to-day details. This is a friendship with trust deep enough to admit that not only do you feed your kids bologna, but that you buy enough of it that when your friend sees it on sale, she calls to tell you so you can speed over to that grocery store and stock up before they sell out. Friendship at this level of life connection occurs only when you live close enough to drive the same streets, feel the same rainstorm, and hear the same stories, while at the same time vigorously guarding each other's hearts and souls. On my worst parenting day ever, when shame threatened to overtake me, it was Lisa, my "bologna is on sale" friend, whom I called. She was the one who reminded me that my mistakes did not define me. To be that kind of soul sister, you have to share the same big values and be willing to speak the truth, even when it's hard, and sit in silence, even when it's uncomfortable. As a group of friends, we sat with each other through funerals, cancer diagnoses, relationship struggles, and babies in the NICU. We celebrated birthdays, baby showers, new jobs, and promotions together. We laughed and cried in equal measure, and I wish I'd appreciated then how easy Lisa had made it for me to transition to that new life and find my people.

When we drove away from North Carolina to our new duty station in Virginia, I cried like a baby. I knew I'd never find another group of friends like that one. And I was right—the new group of friends I made in Virginia was nothing like the one in North Carolina, but it was just as good. In our new assignment, Uncle Sam was my seed friend. Close neighbors became close friends within days of arrival.

Our Fort Belvoir housing assignment (based on Drew's rank and number of children) handed me a group of friends the same age, in the same stage of life, with the same family size and values, living on the same street! My new "bologna is on sale" friends literally lived right next door. Our identical houses were wrapped tightly around a small loop, so we stared directly into one another's windows—and lives—without even trying. You can keep few secrets when you live that close to one another. I knew exactly when everyone on the loop put their trash out, what time their lights turned on or off, what their spouse did at work, when they left each morning, and how stressed they were based on the number of wine bottles in the recycling bin. It was small-town America, in the best of ways. We spent hours sitting in front yards talking about life, even when days were hard. After three years, I cried like a baby again as we drove away from Virginia toward our new NASA life in Texas.

This pain is temporary, I told myself. *You've done this before. Life may be lonely at first, but within a matter of days, or a couple of weeks at most, your "bologna is on sale" friends will appear, and everything will be good again . . . right?*

✳   ✳   ✳

I was still weeping into my steering wheel in the YMCA parking lot when Lisa answered my call on the second ring. I howled about how alone I was, how drained I was, how jealous I was of Drew having friends while I had none, and how I wished we had never moved to Texas. She listened like a good friend does, but then she did what only great friends do—she challenged me.

"I don't have any friends!" I whined.

"I know that's hard," she said. "What are you going to do about it?"

That simple question changed everything.

Her question made me realize that, up to that moment, I had been living as if I expected someone else to create my relationships for me, the way Lisa had done in North Carolina and the way the US Army had done through our housing assignment in Virginia. I realized I had been living as if one day the phone would ring and I'd hear an unfamiliar but incredibly friendly voice on the other end. "Hello," she'd say. "You don't know me, but I am an amazing person and I hear you are an amazing person too. Would you like to be best friends forever?" I'd happily accept. Fast-forward twenty years, and our kids would marry each other and we'd spend all our summer vacations together.

Deep down, I knew that's not how adult female friendships work, but my actions said otherwise. I was living in a friendship fantasyland, and my overwhelming loneliness was testament to its falsehood. Lisa's question forced me to face the reality that if I wanted to be surrounded by a community of "bologna is on sale" friends, it was up to me to do something about it.

So I made a plan. Every Wednesday for the next three months, I reserved 9 a.m. to noon on my schedule. I planned to invite a different woman over for coffee each week. Even after six months in Texas, I didn't actually *know* twelve women, so that meant I had to approach all the friendly women I'd been eyeballing at church, at the preschool, at the gym, or in my neighborhood, and ask for their number. The first few times I stumbled over my words, worried about rejection or sounding desperate.

"Hey, would you like to have coffee sometime? What's your number? I can text you." *Oh no*, I'd think. *Am I the mom equivalent of a sleazy guy in a bar asking for your number?*

Though my self-assurance and energy faltered a few times, the smiles and happy exchange of digits from each woman I talked to gave me the confidence I needed to keep it up.

"Tomorrow's Wednesday! Or as I like to call it, Friendsday!" Drew would jokingly declare while we brushed our teeth on Tuesday night. "Who's coming over tomorrow?"

"Oh, I don't know," I'd mumble between rinses. "It's supposed to be Susan, but I think she's going to flake on me. Who cares?"

"Who cares?" Drew would say. "I care! You need friends, and these coffee dates are great! Afterward you always tell me what a good time it was. I'm not letting you give up. Text Susan in the morning and tell her you're looking forward to seeing her."

"Okay," I'd say, secretly happy someone was continuing to push me outside my comfort zone.

Each week I texted another woman, asking if she wanted to come over the following Wednesday. If she couldn't that week, I'd ask about the next week, or if she couldn't come that week either, the week after that. I was persistent, actively pursuing connection in a way I never had before. Over the next few months, all twelve women came over to hang out, many of them expressing excitement about being asked into my home rather than a local coffee shop. Most of these women seemed like me, longing for female friends but endlessly waiting for someone else to make the first move. Each Wednesday morning was a scheduled blind date, complete with some sparkling conversations I never wanted to end and some fizzling disappointments that dragged across the finish line. But by the end of my round robin, a few gems sparkled in my hand, women with whom I had a real connection and who became invaluable "seed friends," introducing me to other circles of women I could meet and try to find connection with.

Friendship is hard work. Sometimes that's easy to forget since established circles of friends make it look so effortless, at least from a distance. But in my experience, finding authentic, trustworthy friends is one of the most difficult and universal challenges adult women face, made doubly hard by how painful it is to admit the depth of our longing for it, even to ourselves.

In seasons where friendship has felt scarce, I've told myself, *Maybe loneliness is simply part of what it is to be an adult woman*, while simultaneously boiling in jealousy toward women who never seem to be alone. I've picked up the heavy rocks of my anger and disappointment from past friendship burns, grief over lost companions, and fear of my own isolation, thrown them into my emotional backpack, and attempted to hike the treacherous paths of life alone. The outcome is always the same: I may move forward for a while, but I'm eventually forced to stop, brought to my knees by the weight of the burdens I attempt to carry on my own.

If Drew's deployments and time in space taught me anything, it's that we are not designed to experience this life alone. Celebrations and suffering are meant to be shared. We are hardwired to find safety and purpose in the companionship of others. The unique type of companionship that is found only in the bonds of female friendship cannot be replicated or replaced with something else. Even the best of marriages, the most delightful of children, the most fulfilling work or home life, or the most caring parents cannot fill the friend-shaped space God carved into our hearts. God plants this longing in us for a purpose. He knows life is hard. He knows that the same blue sky that is full of sun today may be darkened by a whirling tornado tomorrow, and that without friends to cling to, it's easy to get blown away. God straight up calls us to find "bologna is on sale" friends:

If either of them falls down,
>one can help the other up.
But pity anyone who falls
>and has no one to help them up.

Also, if two lie down together, they will keep warm.
But how can one keep warm alone?
Though one may be overpowered,
two can defend themselves.
A cord of three strands is not quickly broken.
ECCLESIASTES 4:10-12

Without caring friends around us, we may survive hard seasons, but that's all we'll do. As the writer of the passage from Ecclesiastes implies, picking ourselves up when we fall, especially when we're carrying a heavy emotional backpack, can be darn near impossible. When we are alone, our metaphorical nights are cold, and we feel unprotected and weak. But with a friend at our side to laugh, cry, and shoulder our burdens with, we can move confidently through tough times, knowing God placed this person in our lives to journey alongside us. Even when life is hard, a good friend helps keep you on the right path and reminds you to choose hope when fear threatens to overtake you.

My Texas friendship struggles illuminated the fact that finding and maintaining "bologna is on sale" girlfriends must be an active, intentional, and continuous pursuit. Every time I hesitated to put myself out there, I reminded myself: It was the *people* who had made life so meaningful, so fulfilling, and so wonderful everywhere we lived. If I wanted to thrive in this new life, I needed to *find my people*. To fill the friend-shaped hole in my heart, I had to put aside my fear of rejection, shallow judgments I'd made about my new community, and basic misunderstandings about how to make friends, and I had to double down on my friendship investments.

When I embraced the fact that finding friends must be an active pursuit, I began prioritizing friendships as I had in the past, asking women to spend quality time with me and saying yes whenever I could to their invitations. I left space in my schedule. I forced myself to be open to talking about our experiences in the Army and honest about our current experiences at NASA. And I kept my eyes focused up and out, searching for women who looked as lost as I once was, open to the possibility that every new friendship was a potential best friend.

Finding your people can be a struggle. You have to be intentional, thoughtful, and vigilant. Being a good friend is hard work. But it's a sacred, purposeful undertaking.

* * *

Six years after our move to Houston, I sit in mission control with two of my closest friends, women I have trusted with the deepest, darkest, most sensitive parts of myself. At this point, it's hard to remember how low I felt those first six months in Texas. Catie and Allison are the "bologna is on sale" friends I need, especially today. Catie knows that my calm and sometimes aloof exterior hides a nervousness and need for reassurance I don't often verbalize, so as the spacewalk progresses, she asks the questions she knows I should hear the answers to.

"Everything's going great, right? Is this the best spacewalk you've ever seen?" she asks the flight director. When he laughs and answers in the affirmative, she turns and winks at me with a sly grin.

In response, I crack a joke about how boring the day was. "We have to eat all these chips before the day wraps up," I say to my escort, "so make sure you give me a good thirty-minute heads-up so I can stuff them all in my mouth before we leave."

Allison, who sits next to me, knows I often use quick jokes to hide my feelings of vulnerability or as clumsy attempts at connection, so she presses her shoulder against mine. "Thanks for inviting me to be here today," she says. "This is awesome. I'm so glad I could experience this with you." We've done life together long enough to know that experiencing this moment together is what I need most from her. I press my shoulder back into hers.

This won't be my last time sitting in mission control with my friends. Over the next eight months, Drew will complete six more spacewalks, an uncommonly high number for one single mission. Each EVA morning will begin with the same flustering dance of kid management, NASA TV, cereal bowls, backpacks, and school buses. But in the midst of the morning chaos, I always feel at peace, knowing that soon I'll be sitting with my friends again, nervously watching Drew and his crewmates do the impossible and confident that no matter what happens, I'm not alone.

CHAPTER 3

HOUSTON, WE HAVE A BIRTHDAY!

GET COMFORTABLE WITH VULNERABILITY

July 17, 2019

Baikonur, Kazakhstan

After our four-hour flight from Moscow to Kazakhstan, my kids and I are waiting to clear immigration in a remote Kazakh airport on the outskirts of Baikonur. The agent's suspicious eyes flick between my kids' faces and their passport photos. The worker doesn't look much older than Daniel. His older, stern-looking supervisor hovers over his shoulder, double-checking his work.

"Stand still and be quiet," I whisper to the kids. "Just stay here next to me where the officials can see you."

There's a poster on the wall next to us, reminding the reader that attempting to bribe immigration officials is a serious crime. It's written in Russian, but the sentiment expressed is clear. The kids notice it and poke me, asking what it means.

"I'll explain later," I say. "Let's get out of here first."

The longer this document examination takes, the more nervous I become and the worse I feel that our family group of five is slowing the line. Behind us are the fifty people who were on the Russian charter flight with us. The air-conditioning is blasting, but I'm sweating and I can feel my shirt sticking to my back. My escort is behind us in line, subtly monitoring our progress and poised to step in with some well-placed Russian phrases of explanation if there's an issue with our documents. After several minutes of minimal observable activity, the agent suddenly stamps our paperwork and slides our passports back to us in a thick bundle. I grab them and stuff them into my bag as I herd the kids toward the baggage claim area. I nod to my escort; over his shoulder I can see our invited guests lined up, patiently waiting their turns, each clutching their carry-on bag and passport, politely shuffling as the person in front of them moves forward.

* * *

Choosing who would wait with me in this tiny airport in the middle of nowhere was no easy task. To witness Drew's launch in person, we would have to travel halfway around the globe and into a completely different world. Drew and I were given fifteen spots for the launch, but after the five spots for the kids and me, we could bring only ten guests along. As the deadline to submit the guests' names and contact information loomed, we wrestled to finalize our list of invitees. Between our Houston friends, twenty years of military friends, and a family tree full of parents, siblings, aunts, uncles, and cousins, we had dozens of people to consider.

"We have to hurry up and make our decision," one of us would say every time we looked at our scrawled list of possibilities.

"I know!" the other would whine. "Let's just sleep on it one more night."

One piece of advice kept bubbling up from every experienced astronaut family we talked to: Invite only people you can count on to support you well, because you'll need it. Sure, if everything goes smoothly, a rocket launch is a joyous occasion that should generate excitement and be celebrated. But traveling to the other side of the world can also be incredibly stressful. This trip was made all the more complicated by four kids, family dynamics, hot weather, jet lag, the language barrier, and a lack of tourist amenities. I needed companions who understood their essential role as helpers, both for travel logistics and emotional support. The ten-day length of the trip and the high price tag each guest had to pay were other variables we had to consider, so it took Drew and me six months to finalize our invite list. We fully understood that the honor of being offered one of these ten coveted spots might be overshadowed by the time away from home or work and the financial sacrifice required.

We were astonished and delighted when all ten of our first-choice invitees excitedly accepted our invitation. Drew's parents, his two brothers, my mom, my friend Lisa and her husband, and three of Drew's Army buddies agreed to accompany us. They immediately began filling out reams of confusing paperwork for passports, Russian visas, plane tickets, hotel reservations, and trip itineraries without the NASA support team taking care of it for them as they did for our immediate family. Just completing the process to leave the country was a meaningful offering of love and support to us, and the first plane hadn't even cleared the runway yet.

* * *

As the kids and I wait for our entire group to clear immigration, I'm reminded why I prefer fast and light adventure travel, with just Drew as my companion. In years past we stuffed a few days' worth of clothes into shoulder bags and trekked through mountains in Switzerland, fjords in Norway, and hidden coves in Mexico. We perfected our nebulous tourist look, secretly thrilled when area residents assumed we were Canadian, European, or best of all, locals like them. We planned every aspect of our trip—eating where the locals eat, sleeping in unique houses or hostels, and never doing the same thing twice.

This trip is the opposite in every way. The kids and I have several huge suitcases stuffed with more clothes, shoes, snacks, and books than we really need. Between my guests, the guests of the other crew members, and a plethora of NASA employees, we're a huge group of Americans who stand out wherever we go. Almost every hour over the next four days before the launch has been scheduled for our gaggle of fifteen, and we will rarely be more than an arm's length away from one another. Our hotel rooms are next to each other in the same hotel wing. We'll eat together at the same table in the same restaurant for almost every meal. We'll squeeze together in the same vehicles, going to the same places to experience the same things. We'll move like a throng of astronaut Drew Morgan groupies, snapping thousands of pictures and asking hundreds of questions, often while wearing matching T-shirts. I haven't traveled in a group this large since my high school band trip to Disney World, and as I glance back at the tired but smiling faces of our family and friends trickling into baggage claim, I wonder if all the togetherness may get old fast.

By the time we're ready to leave the airport, the jet lag and my underlying stress about the launch has me primed for annoyance. Just when I'm about to snap at the kids to help with the suitcases, my escort swoops in to snag a bag and a friend grabs another. As we head outside to load our luggage under the bus, the blast of 100-degree heat in the parking lot gives us a jolting reminder that we're not in temperate Moscow anymore. Several relatives call out to the kids, inviting them to sit in the back of the bus with them, allowing me the unexpected pleasure of sitting next to a friend.

"Are you ready for this?" Lisa asks as the bus pulls away from the airport.

"I don't know what to be ready for," I respond.

"Well, whatever you need, you just tell us. We're here for you," she replies.

Drew has spent the last two weeks in Baikonur with his crewmates and support team. The astronauts are strictly quarantined in a small cluster of buildings behind barbed wire and tight security. Only a handful of authorized personnel are allowed any kind of face-to-face interaction with the crew. The astronauts and cosmonauts are not allowed to leave the facility and are rarely left alone. Food is carefully prepared on site and Russian doctors hover nearby, watching to make sure protocols are maintained. The health of the crew is of paramount importance. But now that training, testing, and inspections are over, there is little to help them pass the time. All that's left is the count-down to launch, so Drew has been anxiously awaiting our arrival. We're just as anxious to see him.

The days leading up to the launch are a tightly choreographed dance of activities. And I'm reminded over and over that my friend's promise to do whatever I needed has been fulfilled, not only by her but by the other family members and friends. All day, the kids are handed off for a game of cards with a friend, a swim in the pool with our escort, or a walk around the hotel with a grandparent. Except when we're in the van or visiting Drew together, I don't even know how the kids are spending their time or who is feeding them each meal. Every night after dinner I have the opportunity to visit Drew alone, which is great, but that means someone else has to put the kids to bed, no simple task since they are spread out in three different hotel rooms. A grandparent happily takes on the duty, and by the time I return late each night, they are all asleep. I can feel that my guests are giving me space, both physically and emotionally. They can see that I'm a bit overwhelmed by the upcoming launch and these recurring, draining goodbyes with Drew.

Every day we have an opportunity to visit Drew in the quarantine facility press conference room, talking to him behind thick glass. The first day, the kids and I pull our chairs up as close as possible to the glass, using a microphone to talk with him through the speaker system. Drew pulls his chair up inches from the glass on the other side, but now that the crew's prelaunch work is complete, he has no new information to share. The kids have little to say once they finish telling Drew what they did earlier in the day, which doesn't take long either. As our conversation wanes, it feels more like we're observing a gorilla at the zoo rather than visiting with Drew. We take some selfies to kill some time. Sophia and Gabby pretend to sing karaoke into the microphones. We talk about what we're having for lunch. We stare at each other. Exciting stuff.

On the second day, we bring our guests along. They ask plenty of questions, and their excitement is a great distraction from the looming launch countdown.

"What have you been doing with yourself these past couple days?" Drew's dad asks him.

"Not much. Exercising, doing some email. They took pictures of our crew playing Ping-Pong, billiards, and chess together yesterday, which is a strange tradition they do with every crew," Drew replies.

"Do you have to make your own food? How does that work?" Drew's brother asks.

"Nah, there are people here who cook for us. It's traditional Russian and Kazakh food, but it's pretty good. I like it. When we were here in late November for training, the cooks attempted an American Thanksgiving dinner. While it wasn't exactly right, it was really thoughtful of them to try, and not too bad!"

After visiting with Drew, our group explores the local market, smelling the piles of exotic spices and examining the variety of camel hide products. We try on traditional Kazakh-style hats and laugh at the juxtaposition of local handicrafts and space-themed merchandise for sale. In every merchant's stall is a section dedicated to Expedition 60 swag, with magnets and other trinkets featuring a picture of the crew in their space suits, piled up for easy purchase. One friend buys a shirt with Drew's face printed on the front.

The third day we drive onto the Cosmodrome property to watch the Soyuz rocket travel via train car from the assembly hangar to the launchpad. After a forty-minute drive, our bus pulls off the old, crumbling road and into a sprawling, potholed parking lot. As I step outside, I can see radio towers and a cluster of buildings in the far distance across the flat landscape, but it's the streams of people that make me gasp. This is our first interaction with the space tourists, and the sheer number is astonishing. Where did they all come from? They seem to be pouring endlessly out of buses and vans like clowns from a fleet of circus cars. After jumping out of their vehicles, they run up the street toward a set of train tracks that meander along the road and extend into the hazy distance. The tourist hustle makes our group move more urgently as we join their throng. We head toward a single yellow rope strung along the railway, staked up to keep everyone back. Once we find an empty spot along the rope, the train track only about fifty yards in front of us, we crane our necks and see a smudge of green and black slowly creeping toward us. My escort tells us it's the rocket, and while there are less than two miles of track separating the assembly hangar and the launchpad, the rocket's short trip will take almost two hours. As I look at the long loop of track it needs to cover and its unhurried 3 mph travel speed, I can hardly imagine that it will ever pass us.

It's considered bad luck for the crew to watch their own rocket roll out, but when I gaze down the rope line, I see the backup crew—easily recognizable in their bright blue flight suits—walking along the tracks.

"Tom! Hey, Tom!" I call out. Astronaut Tom Marshburn is Drew's backup and good friend. I wave as he looks my way and heads over.

"How are you? Is everything going well?" he asks.

"Yes, thanks," I say. By now the tourists have noticed Tom near us at the rope line and start squeezing in, elated to see a real astronaut up close. They start peppering Tom with questions and snapping pictures. The politest guy I know, he patiently answers their questions and poses for pictures from a safe distance. As he does, Drew's green Soyuz rocket creeps closer and closer on the tracks, eventually rolling by in front of us, slowly enough that the Russian security guards easily keep up as they stroll alongside it. The rocket is on its side, lying on a specially designed train car that will roll right up to the base of the launchpad and then hoist the rocket into the vertical position, ready for launch. I've never seen a Soyuz rocket in person before. It's smaller than I expected, and the shiny green paint glitters in the sunlight. Like the tourists around us, we pull out our phones and start recording video and snapping selfies. The rocket rolls on past us, the locomotive and its single rocket-bearing, flatbed train car chugging toward the launchpad.

The combination of Tom in his blue flight suit and the rocket rolling behind him spins the tourists into a level of frantic excitement we rarely see for the space program back in the States. Their enthusiasm is gratifying and contagious, but I'm feeling a little crushed, so

I step back from the rope line and wave goodbye to Tom. As I turn, for a brief moment I see him, not as I usually do—a regular guy and my friend—but as the tourists do, a brave hero in a blue NASA flight suit, willing to risk his life to push the boundaries of human space exploration.

Though our schedule is somewhat relaxed between official activities, nothing is simple. The extreme heat makes spending time outside almost unbearable, and staying hydrated is a serious concern. We're told we shouldn't drink the tap water, so we have to carry large bottles of water wherever we go. The local food is delicious, but the menu is limited, and we have to be careful about the food safety of local fruits and vegetables. Simmering underneath it all, for me at least, is the pool of angst that grows with each hour that brings us closer to the big event. I feel myself becoming more overwhelmed, like there's a giant ticking clock in my head. To deal with the stress, I can feel myself curling up emotionally and withdrawing into myself—much different from my usual open, gregarious personality.

As we sit down for lunch, a friend asks me what I want to order.

"Ah, I don't know. Same as yesterday, I guess. The plov." Plov is a meat and rice dish so common on every Baikonur menu that it's become a running joke. We've all eaten it so many times in the past few days that we're completely sick of it. Yet the thought of actually reading the menu and picking something different feels harder than forcing myself to eat the same meal again.

Once the dish arrives, it just sits in front of me slowly congealing. I'm not really that hungry, but I don't feel up for small talk either. I feel tired and anxious, and if I'm really honest, bloated from all the plov I had the day before. In between forced bites, I chime into conversation where appropriate, but I'm just dialing it in. My mind is preoccupied with the goodbye the kids and I had with Drew that morning behind the glass at our daily family visit, the goodbye I will say again when I see Drew briefly tonight, and how we will do it all again tomorrow. It's emotionally exhausting. Every aspect of this trip and its unfamiliar level of stress has me off-kilter. I'm not in control of anything, and I'm nervous about the future. My uneasiness and disengagement do not go unnoticed by my guests.

When I wake up one morning, I realize I am alone in my quiet hotel room. I'd taken a sleeping pill the night before because the stress was making it hard for my brain to turn off. Apparently the pill knocked me out so cold that I hadn't heard Sophia, the child sharing the room with me, as she got up and dressed before leaving the room, which is mildly concerning. I look at my phone and see a text from my family.

"The kids have eaten breakfast and are playing supervised by the pool." I respond with a thumbs-up emoji. Another text dings. It's from my mom.

"They are about to close breakfast in the restaurant. Do you want a coffee?"

What time is it? I wonder. Between the blackout curtains and that sleeping pill, I have completely lost all sense of time. I haven't been this out of it since I had my last baby eight years ago.

"Yes, a coffee please!!!" I text back. I open the curtains and jump in the shower. When I get out ten minutes later, two coffees are sitting on my side table, made just the way I like them, along with a few pieces of fruit. I eat them slowly while I get dressed and mentally prepare myself for another day of visiting Drew, saying goodbye again, and killing time.

Today, like every day on this trip, my group has surrounded me and is taking care of everything. I haven't had to manage an itinerary, feed a single child, take out my wallet, or make a hard decision since we left the United States. I haven't been this well cared for in . . . well . . . ever. A little voice in the back of my mind reminds me that I've never actually *let* someone care for me like this before.

I feel exposed and more than a little vulnerable. It's probably an understatement to say I don't usually need a lot of help.

A few hours later, the kids and I are told to sit in the front row at the international press conference. The Soyuz crew, all sporting their blue flight suits, colorful mission patches, and fresh haircuts, smile and wave behind the now-familiar, thick glass window wall in front of us while the press squeezes in behind, their cameras clicking in friendly machine-gun bursts. The reporters ask both the standard questions and some hilarious random queries.

"Drew, this is your first flight. How do you feel?"

"Aleksandr, you have an international crew. Tell us about how you work together."

"Luca, are you aware that you are very popular with Russian women on social media? Why do you think that is?"

While answering one question, Drew wishes Amelia a happy birthday—she turns thirteen today. He repeats his birthday wishes in Russian, and the press titters in delight at witnessing this personal moment. Sitting next to her, I can feel her adolescent embarrassment bloom, but the smile she and Drew share overcomes her mild discomfort.

Before the trip, she and I decided we'd celebrate her birthday when we got home, just to make things easier. My logical, practical child readily agreed, so in all my preparations for the trip, I completely put her birthday out of my mind after that. Fast-forward a few weeks and I'm cursing my lack of birthday foresight. At lunch, our entire group heads to a local restaurant, a standard part of the trip itinerary for the day before the launch. As I look at Amelia across the table, I remember the day thirteen years earlier when I held her in my arms for the first time. Sitting in the restaurant empty-handed, my mom guilt is working overtime and I am overwhelmed with remorse. I could have at least brought a small gift with me to commemorate her big day, but it completely slipped my mind in all the trip planning. I've done nothing, brought nothing, to celebrate her. What kind of mother am I? I can barely look at the birthday girl as I choke down another plate of plov, I'm so disappointed in myself.

Just when I feel as if I'll never be able to crawl out from under this crushing pile of shame, a sound catches my attention.

"Is it time for the surprise?"

"Let's bring it out now!"

"Happy thirteenth birthday!"

I stare across the room as our server brings out the most beautiful birthday cake any thirteen-year-old-girl could imagine. It's a confectionary masterpiece, covered with swirls of white icing and clusters of green-striped fruits that look like tiny, round watermelons. She places it in front of Amelia, who grins sheepishly.

I look over at my escort. "I know you mentioned something about a cake for her birthday, but where in the world did you get that?" I whisper.

"I had some help," he replies with a wink.

Our fellow diners applaud for the birthday girl, and my jaw drops even further as friends and family pull out gifts from under the table—a bouquet of flowers, a leather-tooled jewelry box purchased during our trip to the local market.

As we begin to sing "Happy Birthday," the people at the table behind us turn around and join in, their enthusiastic voices thick with Russian, Italian, and French accents. Together, we create the most rousing chorus of the song I've ever heard. My daughter is smiling from ear to ear, clearly delighted at this unexpected turn of events. I couldn't have orchestrated a more unique and meaningful birthday celebration if I had tried, and the thoughtfulness and love reflected in this extraordinary moment brings me to tears. My heart is full, knowing that despite my parenting failure, Amelia will have this exceptional memory for the rest of her life.

Letting other people handle the responsibilities, forgetting birthdays, crying because my heart is full of appreciation—this is not how I normally live. Because I take great pride in handling things by myself, allowing people to step into my life in this intimate way makes me feel emotionally naked. I realize as I wade into this uncharted territory that I am uncomfortable and yet inexplicably comforted at the same time. Acknowledging my limits is clearly not something I do well, but for this week at least, I have no choice. I need help, and my friends and family are happily offering it. I think it's time I got comfortable with being vulnerable.

* * *

The first time I recognized the bravery it takes to open our lives to others came when we lived in Virginia. I met Jennifer and Amber within my first week there. Our three identical houses formed a triangle across our tight cul-de-sac, our front doors directly facing each other. Our friendship bond formed quickly, and even though there were only six houses on the street, at one point thirty-three children called this tiny loop home. It was a raucous place to live, with any number of kids at any given time riding their bikes around the circle, climbing fences, or exploring the old woods. Amber, Jennifer, and I sat outside and talked while the kids played, hung out together at night, and walked together on weekends. I recruited both of them to join the MOPS moms group I started on post, and they jumped in and became two of my most dedicated leaders. We spent hours together each week, both casually socializing and purposefully working on projects as a ministry team. I had found my people, and I loved every minute of it.

About a year after we'd connected, Amber's husband, Richard, left for a nine-month deployment to Afghanistan. Two months later, Amber delivered baby number five. To our civilian friends, this unfortunate timing was a travesty. To those of us who had spent the better part of a decade attempting to time births between deployment cycles, this was just how it was. We all had friends who had given birth alone while their husbands, stationed in a remote location, watched the birth of their child via Skype. If your husband was able to physically be in the room for the birth of all your children, you counted yourself lucky. Doubly unlucky for Amber, with the iPad set up and ready to connect with Richard on the day of her delivery, there was a communications blackout, not an unusual occurrence for troops in combat zones. So Amber delivered her baby with only her sister-in-law and Jennifer by her side. Her husband met the new baby via videoconference the next day. We all agreed that it wasn't the ideal set of circumstances, but it wasn't the end of the world, either. A few days after her delivery, we welcomed Amber and the new baby back to the loop and life moved on. All was well, or so we thought.

A month or so after the baby came home, I noticed something that gave me pause. Amber's trash cans were full, and no one had pulled them to the curb. Not a big deal, but something that hadn't happened before in all the weeks Richard had been gone. A few nights later, I was up unusually late one evening when I happened to look out my window and saw something surprising: All the lights on the second floor of Amber's house were on. Because my house was identical to hers, I knew that not only were the lights in the master bedroom on, but those in her kids' rooms as well. I stood by the window, pondering this strange turn of events.

What could possibly be going on over there at midnight? I wondered. *I hope the baby isn't sick or keeping Amber up all night. And why are all the lights on? It's a school night and the other kids should be in bed. This doesn't make any sense. Should I text her and make sure everything is okay?*

I rocked back and forth on my heels as I considered going downstairs to fetch my cell phone and send her a message. I shook my head, my own hesitation and the effort to walk downstairs too much to overcome in the moment.

Yet as I lay back down in my bed, a small gnawing feeling began to grow within me. Something wasn't right.

The feeling didn't go away. A dozen red flags appeared during conversations with her kids or when I looked into Amber's eyes. She looked fine during our moms' group. At our meetings Amber was showered with her hair brushed and makeup on, laughing and happy. She didn't look like the stereotype of a struggling mom, but deep down, because our lives were so intertwined, I knew something wasn't right. Each little warning signal felt like a divine tap on my shoulder, with God whispering, "Did you see that?" into my ear. I couldn't deny that something felt off, but I honestly didn't know what to do about it. Surely Amber would tell us if something was wrong. She was a former US Marine, for goodness' sake. If I shared my concerns with her—a strong, independent, low-maintenance woman—I'd seem nosy and doubtful of her ability to care for her own family. She'd probably be insulted, and it would irreparably damage our relationship. Our friendship was too valuable for me to risk it, so I did nothing. My justification for inaction ran on a continuous loop in my head:

She'd tell me if she needed help.
If she was really struggling, she'd look more haggard than she does.
Just wait for her to come to you.
It's none of your business.
I'm sure everything is fine.

But over the following weeks, my discomfort grew. Every time I passed a window, I would look out and see something that concerned me. Her kids were outside at strange hours, and lights were on too early in the morning and too late at night. Passing comments by Amber—about how difficult the kids were being, how messy the house was, or how stressed her teenager was making her—pricked at my conscience and made my internal discomfort unbearable. My nightly prayer was simple: "God, tell me what to do."

In my gut, I knew what he wanted me to do; I just needed to summon the courage to do it. So one afternoon I headed across the street. The last few feet felt like a mile as I climbed the top step and knocked on Amber's door. We usually just tapped quickly and waltzed right in like we owned the place. Waiting for her to answer the door made what I was about to do feel even more serious. I felt nervous standing on her front stoop, not sure if I was about to ruin one of the best friendships I'd ever had. Amber opened the door, baby in her arms.

"Hi," I said. "Can I come inside and talk to you?"

I could tell from the look on her face that my formal request had her concerned.

"Okaaaaay," she said as I stepped inside and we headed down the hallway.

What I saw when I walked into the living room stopped me cold. The room was a mess, and not the kind of "I'm so sorry that my house is a mess" description women use when you walk into their house and find a single magazine thrown on the floor. There was stuff everywhere. Toys, books, papers, clothes, even items that looked like they belonged in the garage were tossed all over the living room floor. We cleared off a space on the couch and sat down, daytime TV flickering on the other side of the room. I wiped my sweaty palms on the thighs of my pants as I turned my body toward Amber and began the opening statement I'd practiced several times in my head.

"I'm not sure what's going on, but I feel like something is wrong. I'm your friend and I love you, and I need to know if something isn't right."

My words rolled out sounding more measured and calm than I felt on the inside. I pressed my hands between my legs while I waited for her reaction.

Amber looked at me for a long moment, breathing slowly as she assessed my sincerity. Then she took a deep breath, dropped her head, and began to cry. In between sobs she laid out what life had been like the last few weeks since the baby had arrived. Her teenage daughter, whom Amber had been counting on to help, was creating more stress than support. The other three kids, between the ages of four and eight, were running wild. They were calling the shots, and not in an adorable "Let's put on a puppet show" kind of way. It was more of a *Lord of the Flies* situation, and the chaos in the living room was just the first hint of it. Bedtimes were like a prison riot. Disrespect and disobedience were rampant. Mealtimes were a nightmare. Like all moms with a newborn, Amber was mentally and physically exhausted. Instead of helping, or at least not making things worse, it was as if the other four kids were conspiring to drive her insane. To say that Amber was drowning would be an understatement. She was done and had already sunk to the bottom. She needed more than a life preserver; she needed CPR. When she was done talking, I leaned forward, resting my elbows on my knees.

"Okay," I said, looking in her eyes. "I love you and I want to help you. And when I say I want to help you, I'm not talking about bringing dinner over or just praying for you. Those things are important, but I'm talking about something else. Do you need me to come over here and be the bad guy to help right this ship?"

She looked at me for another long moment. "Yes. Yes, I do."

"Okay," I said. "Have the kids here on the couch at 4 p.m. today. You tell them there's a new sheriff in town."

I walked out Amber's front door and headed straight over to Jennifer's house, letting myself in. I found her in the kitchen. "Saddle up, Jennifer. Amber's in trouble."

I recounted everything Amber had told me, and Jennifer was equally concerned and primed for action. We made a plan and agreed to meet at Amber's house a few hours later to activate it.

Promptly at 4 p.m., Jennifer and I threw open Amber's front door, startling the kids she'd herded into the living room.

"Listen up!" I said as I slapped a paper up on the wall. I was going for a purposefully intimidating combination of Martin Luther, General Patton, and Mary Poppins.

"We love your mom, and she needs help, so we are here to do just that. You guys are supposed to be helping too, but instead you've been making things harder." I gave a long, hard side-eye to the sixteen-year-old.

"To get things back on track, here are the new rules we will be enforcing, starting now." I pointed to the paper on the wall as Jennifer menacingly crossed her arms across her chest and squared her feet on the carpet. "Number one: Everyone sleeps in their own beds. Number two: Everyone eats the same thing for dinner. Number three: Everyone helps. Any questions?"

The kids sat there, staring at us in stunned silence. Amber hovered behind them with the wide, eager eyes of a lottery winner about to be handed a giant check for a million dollars.

"No? Great. Let's start cleaning up this house."

I told Amber to go sit with the baby while the rest of us headed into the kitchen, where the sink was full of dirty dishes and the counters were covered with drink cups and snack wrappers. Jennifer and I moved in tandem like a pair of dancing drill sergeants, barking clear, age-appropriate instructions for each child to follow. The fun and casual moms that Amber's kids knew from neighborhood playtime had clearly left the building, and the look in their eyes made clear that our "shock and awe" campaign was hitting its target. Within minutes, the kids were cleaning off counters and bagging up trash.

After managing the cleanup in the living room, the bathrooms, and the bedrooms upstairs, we gave the kids one more round of instructions before heading downstairs to fill Amber in on our plan. We told her that at least one of us would be there to help facilitate bedtime routines every night until we weren't needed anymore. We'd stay as long as necessary to ensure her kids stayed in their rooms and didn't disturb her so she and the baby could get some much-needed rest. We told her she was to make only one dinner option each night; the kids could take it or leave it. Then Jennifer and I left, high-fiving each other on the way out. We came back at 7 p.m. to make sure the kitchen was clean, teeth were brushed, and all the kids were settled in bed. We reminded Amber of the nighttime rules as we made our way downstairs an hour later.

"You need to be in your room getting ready for bed with the baby by 10 p.m. Lock your door. If any kid comes knocking, do not answer your door unless you smell smoke. Just text us and one of us will come over and deal with it."

And deal with it we did. For the next two months, either Jennifer or I was in her house for bedtime almost every single night. We worked through a few bumps in the road during the first couple of weeks. We brought over night-lights for the boys' room so they wouldn't be scared when we closed the bedroom door. The teenager refused to clean her room, so while she was at school we bagged up everything on her bedroom floor, including her comforter and phone charging cord, and took them to my house. A typical teen, she arrogantly shrugged it off when she got home that day and found her room empty. It took a dead phone battery and a few chilly nights before she showed up at my door, promising to clean her room from then on before I gave it all back to her.

We texted Amber a few times to make sure everything was okay when we saw her lights on too late at night. At times it felt like we were managing a second family, but it was a joy to help her, even if it was a sacrifice, because Amber was one of our people. Her willingness to be so vulnerable, both revealing her failings and accepting help, was extraordinary. Our goal was to stand in the gap until she had enough physical, mental, and emotional margin to take care of her kids and her house on her own, which she eventually did. But in the meantime, Amber never seemed embarrassed about us stepping so deeply into her private life or personal responsibilities.

Those two months changed me. I'd never seen authentic vulnerability like that up close before. Sure, every friendship book I'd ever read talked about being willing to "get messy" or "be open" if you wanted to connect deeply with your friends, but what did that really mean? For the first time, I experienced what those seemingly trite phrases meant in real life, and they were no small things. Jennifer and I literally got messy, scraping dried toothpaste off bathroom floors, hauling trash cans, and picking Play-Doh out of carpet. But we got emotionally messy too, disciplining Amber's children, having hard conversations with her about her limits, and sharing the lonely burden of deployment life. Contrary to the weakness most people think vulnerability exposes, Amber was never stronger in my eyes than when she was honest enough to reach out and grab the helping hand we were offering. She didn't love that she needed our help, but she was wise enough to know that in this season, if she wanted to do more than just barely survive, she didn't really have a choice.

✳ ✳ ✳

Despite the amazing example Amber gave me, I still don't reach out for help well. It's simply not how I do life. It is uncomfortable to give up my spot as the primary caregiver to my children, not to mention the schedule planner, meal provider, entertainment director, and wholly self-sufficient woman I usually am.

Now in Kazakhstan, my inner critic works overtime:

These are your children, so they are your responsibility. You
shouldn't need this much help with your own kids.
You've already asked these people to sacrifice so much to be here with
you. You can't ask them to do more!
What's the big deal? You're not special; plenty of other astronaut
spouses have done this before. You're not the first and you won't
be the last.
Quit being so emotional. You're being high-maintenance and just
making things harder for everyone.
You invited these people with you on this trip, but you're not being
much of a hostess.
Plenty of people single parent and have hard lives. Your stress is
nothing compared to other people's real stress.
You chose this life; you knew this would happen. You made your
bed, now you have to lie in it.

It's hard to battle the shame and discomfort that constantly bubble up, but once I let go of my pride and let my people see my vulnerabilities, something shifts inside me. Of course I need help. That is clear to everyone. My people circle the wagons around me for ten days, caring for me—not out of obligation or guilt, but out of love. Their generosity of spirit flows out in everything they do, whether helping to haul luggage, keep my kids occupied, or just sit with me when I look nervous. And they help me squash the lies rattling around in my head and replace them with the truth.

Sure, these are your kids. But the old saying is true, it does take a village. It's not irresponsible to need help.
These people love you and want to help you.
This is a big deal, and every launch is different. It's okay to feel overwhelmed.
Expressing deep emotion is healthy. Just because you need help does not make you an overly needy person.
It's not your job to be a hostess all the time. Your people do not expect that of you.
Yes, you have a very blessed life, but that doesn't mean this season is easy.
You are allowed to struggle and need help, even within the choices you've made.

The launch trip is, by far, one of the hardest and most uncomfortable journeys I've ever been on, but at the same time, it's the most impactful exercise in the power of showing vulnerability I've ever experienced. The days are tough, but so full of love and companionship.

When we arrive home after the launch, I find myself mourning the loss of the connections I felt with others in those vulnerable moments. I have tasted the deeper level of trust that comes with vulnerability, and I want that with every person in my life. I vow to not be afraid of being vulnerable with others, so when I swing by my friend Allison's house the day after getting home, I let the tears flow while describing the launch. "Yikes, I really did not expect to get emotional like this when I came over here," I say between nose blows.

"I'm so happy to see this tender side of you," she says as she pulls me into a long embrace, which is just what I need.

As the days turn into weeks and we settle into the new normal, I remind myself that accepting help is not a sign of weakness or bad parenting. I get comfortable with admitting that some days are a struggle and that as capable as I may be, I cannot do it all. In response to my admission, friends practice radical generosity. A friend takes my son out to practice driving several times before his road test. Neighbors drop off small, thoughtful gifts and drive my daughter to volleyball practice. Friends send funny texts to check in on me and gift cards to treat myself on hard days.

A woman from church brings us dinner one Monday night, and as she walks out the door, she asks if this would be a good time for her to bring dinner the following Monday.

"You're going to bring dinner next Monday too?" I ask.

"Oh, I figured I'd bring you guys dinner every Monday while Drew is gone," she says.

My mouth hangs open. "You do know Drew's going to be gone for nine months," I say incredulously.

"Yeah, I know," she says. "When I was a young mom, someone brought me dinner every week during a hard season, and when I told her I'd never be able to repay her, she just smiled and told me to do the same thing for someone else someday. It may have taken me fifty years, but here I am, paying it forward."

And she does—every Monday for nine months. Her generosity takes my breath away, and the breath of every person I tell, as it should.

Vulnerability sounds so simple. Be humble (and realistic), and admit you can't do everything on your own. Let people see your needs. Then let them step up and help you. Admittedly, it's not simple or easy. Old habits and old mindsets die hard. Vulnerability, like hope, is something you have to choose every day. If I had an unofficial motto for difficult times before Drew's launch, it would have been "When the going gets tough, the tough put their heads down and power through it by themselves so they don't inconvenience anyone else."

This mantra was reinforced day after day, year after year, by a culture that values independence above all else and the fact that in my mind, I was so darn good at doing everything all by myself. I would have been better off taking the words of the apostle Peter to heart:

> Above all, love each other deeply, because love covers over a multitude of sins. Offer hospitality to one another without grumbling. Each of you should use whatever gift you have received to serve others, as faithful stewards of God's grace in its various forms.
>
> I PETER 4:8-10

When I read that verse in the past, while firing on all cylinders, I'd think, *Here's the mandate for me to reach out and help others! I'm a high-speed doer, so this is right in my wheelhouse. Brace yourself, friends, because here comes God's grace to you, delivered through me.*

While Drew is gone, on the days I am worn out, frustrated, worried, or at my wits' end, I read this verse very differently. For every giver of love, hospitality, or God's grace in its various forms, there must be a receiver. In this season, at this moment in time, that receiver is me.

Even now, on especially tough days, I remind myself that needing help doesn't make me a failure, weak, or some kind of friendship manipulator. I remind myself that my people want me to be vulnerable because they want to help me when I need it. They reach out not out of obligation or guilt, but because they love me and get as much fulfillment out of it as I do, just as I did with Amber. Sometimes you're the giver and sometimes you're the receiver. Let your people in.

CHAPTER 4

LOST IN SPACE

STAY CONNECTED

March 2020

The kids and I are on a quick spring break trip to Lake Travis, a beautiful lake located in central Texas, when the full reality that life is about to change hits us square in the face.

Drew calls to check in. "Hey, we've been watching the news about COVID-19 up here, and it sounds like things are getting serious."

"Yes, I just watched the news too, and they said the airports are closing. Some schools are closing too!"

"Do you think they'll close our kids' schools?"

"Oh man, let's hope not!"

But, of course, they do close the schools. And my office. And our church. And the coffee shop. And the gym. And all the stores and restaurants.

Prior to the spring of 2020, few people probably thought much about how many other people they saw, talked to, and touched every day. I know I didn't. I calculate that on an average day before the pandemic, I interacted in some way, face-to-face, with at least twenty-five people in a variety of settings:

meetings at work
Sunday church services
coffee with friends
exercise classes at the gym
chance meetings with neighbors in the driveway
the grocery store when offering a polite "excuse me" after
    bumping someone's cart
my front door when smiling at the delivery guy handing me
    my pizza

Connection was something I, and most people, took for granted because it was simply part of how we lived our lives.

As life shifts in this new stay-at-home-order world, I find myself trapped in my house with four adolescent crewmates, none of them as considerate or well behaved as astronauts. Overnight, I gain a new appreciation for Drew's expeditionary skills, the technical name for the soft skills astronauts develop to prepare them to live and work in close quarters with the same people for long periods without killing one another.

"Thank you for picking up your socks, cleaning up after yourself, asking before you borrow things, and for not screaming or crying when you don't get your way," I tell him on the phone. "Of all my crewmates, you're my favorite."

In contrast to my average day here on Earth, Drew interacts face-to-face with only eleven other people during his *entire* nine months in space. The highest number of people on the station with Drew at one time is nine, and that lasts only eight days while a few crews overlap. At one point, only two other astronauts are on the station with Drew. The three of them politely float around each other while they share the living space equivalent of a four-bedroom house. With the lyrics of David Bowie's "Space Oddity" playing in their heads (*Sitting in a tin can / Far above the world*),[7] many people assume that astronauts are experts at isolation.

Is there anything more lonely than orbiting hundreds of miles above the Earth? It's true that astronauts are pros at isolation if that word is defined simply as being physically distant from others. Once the pandemic spread and humanity began to find the four walls of their houses squeezing down on them more and more each day, every news reporter wanted to know: "How do astronauts stay isolated like this for so long? We're going crazy down here on Earth! Tell us your secret!"

The "secret" is no mystery at all. As space missions have gotten longer, astronauts have learned that being isolated is not the same as being alone. Although they may be physically separated from the people they know and love the most, they understand the importance of maintaining connection with the important people in their lives, both face-to-face virtually, by phone, and in other ways. It's a top mission priority, and thanks to COVID-19, most earthbound people now understand why.

As soon as mandatory stay-at-home orders, masks, and social distancing become the new normal, I begin to crave connection in a deeper physical, emotional, and spiritual way than I ever have. I think most people feel the same way. It's simply how we are wired. Our bodies and our souls crave it. In fact, we need it to stay mentally and, for some people, even physically healthy. It's part of what makes us human. We are simply not designed to be alone. As a human race, we've collectively learned what NASA psychologists have known for years—if you want to not just survive challenging and isolating times but to actually come out the other side with your mental health and personal relationships intact, you *must* find ways to stay connected to those you know and love.

✳   ✳   ✳

Our first videoconference with Drew, less than two weeks after he launched into space, is a complete disaster. Ten minutes before the scheduled start time, I gather the kids on the couch, pull out our NASA-issued iPad, look at my instruction sheet, and tap the screen. I'm "calling" the number that will connect me to the console at mission control that will then connect us with Drew.

"Hi! This is John. How do you hear me?" a friendly voice asks from the small iPad speaker.

"Fine. Great. Thanks." I'm not quite sure what the right response is.

"I'm going to go ahead and configure your call. You may see the screen blink a few times; that's normal. We have about nine minutes until the start."

"Oh, okay," I say, now realizing we've got eight and a half minutes to kill before Drew appears. The fussing and crowding begin immediately.

"Stop pushing me!"

"Move over!"

"I can't move over!"

"Yes, you can!"

"Mom, tell her to stop!"

After what seems like an eternity in parenting minutes, a techno ringtone bursts from the iPad, breaking up the fight. After a quick flicker of the screen, Drew appears, a set of headphones on his head, his body floating in the middle of a white module with endless loops of wires, boxes, and switches scattered across the wall behind him.

"Hey, guys! I'm in space! How are you? I miss you!"

The kids are now sitting in frozen silence, staring at the iPad like they've never seen one before.

I pick up the conversation. "Hi, love! You look great! Kids, say hi!"

Silence. I think they've forgotten how to speak English.

"Want me to give you a look around?" Drew asks.

Silence.

Drew tries a new tactic. "What did you think of the launch? How was your flight home from Moscow?"

"It was good," one of the kids mumbles. And it only goes downhill from there.

Drew and I drive the conversation, tossing kid-friendly questions and answers back and forth while Drew gives us a tour around the station.

"I know one of you has to have a question," he finally says. "Maybe something about the food?" More dead air. "Not even anything about the toilet? Everyone wants to know about that."

They answer with awkward shrugs and more shoving, trying to simultaneously scoot close enough to see the screen, while also trying not to touch each other or get touched in return. Gabby starts making weird faces, more interested in watching herself in the corner square of the screen than talking to her dad who is literally doing space somersaults in front of her. We drag the pain on for another thirty minutes before Drew suggests he and I finish the conference alone. I readily agree.

"Well, that was a bust," I say after I've closed the door to our bedroom. "We're going to have to try something else if we're going to do this every weekend for an hour."

"No kidding," Drew replies. "Maybe next time we don't do it all together. But I can already tell that this is going to be a really important part of my week, and I want to stay connected to the kids as much as possible."

"I know," I say. "We'll figure it out."

✳ ✳ ✳

Before his space flight, the longest time Drew had been away from home was during his last deployment to Afghanistan, clocking in at just under eight months. That was ten years and a lifetime ago. At the time, we had three kids, all under the age of six. The youngest wasn't even walking yet. Life wasn't quiet or calm, but it was simple. I didn't work outside the home, so I spent most of each day taking care of the kids and our small house. I wish I could go back in time and tell my younger self to enjoy the innocence and straightforwardness of those days.

While I held down the home front, Drew spent much of his deployment time caring for soldiers in remote locations. Due to the nature of the military mission, we weren't able to talk every day. In fact, we learned that our conversations were better if we didn't talk every day. Every second or third day was just about the right amount of time for us to amass enough interesting tidbits of information to give us something good to discuss. Drew's schedule was flexible enough that he called when he knew I was free.

It was actually easier to involve the kids back then. I connected with Drew through my desktop computer. *Boo beep—boo boo beep.* The Skype audio bubbles would float through my computer speakers. The screen flashed, and there was Drew's face, the metal walls of the shipping container he slept in a familiar background for our video calls. "Hey! How's it going? Where are the kids?"

"Hi! Here's Amelia!" I picked up the squirming, diapered toddler off the floor and held her up in front of the camera. "Say hi to Daddy."

"Hi, Daddy," she said, not even looking at the screen before flopping over boneless and sliding back down to the floor.

"Soph's taking a nap, but here's Daniel." I hoisted our boy up on my lap, and he held out his Thomas the Tank Engine to the camera. Drew asked him a few questions about the toy and school before it became clear that Daniel had lost interest. They said goodbye, and Daniel scampered back downstairs to his waiting toys. His little brain had hardly registered that Drew was gone.

"So what's new?" Drew asked me.

"Just the usual. I'm trying to get Sophia to take longer naps, Amelia's almost convinced it's time to start using the potty, and I'm working on reading with Daniel. Nothing I can't handle."

"I have no doubt. Should we talk about the book?"

"Yeah, let's get into it. I have some big thoughts."

Because we both had free time to fill, we picked out a marriage book and read it together, discussing the next chapter when we talked every week. Absence made the heart grow fonder, and as we pined for each other, we worked though some of our stickiest recurring marital disagreements. It was not as difficult to talk about unhealthy communication patterns, conflicting financial goals, or family baggage with a comfortable seven-thousand-mile buffer between us.

"So I can see how I get a little louder when I feel defensive," I conceded. "I promise to really work on that." It amazed me how much easier it was to admit my own shortcomings when I wasn't ticked about Drew not emptying the dishwasher.

Drew continued our open sharing time. "And I see how I can tend toward criticism. That's not good either. I promise I'll work on that too."

We missed each other so much, we couldn't help but see each other through rose-colored glasses. We wanted to do anything to please each other.

While we both went to bed alone, neither of us was lonely. I had a close group of friends to talk to and share my life with. I was surrounded by women whose husbands were also in Afghanistan, fighting alongside Drew, and we shared in the deployment experience. Drew and a large, constantly shifting group of fellow soldiers supported one another. They moved around from base to base together, patrolling and interacting with locals. There was no lack of connection for either of us. We were separated from each other, but in no way isolated.

* * *

Fast-forward to 2019, and life is very different. We have four children—two teenagers and two tweens. Our schedules are complicated and constantly shifting. Four kids means four different school schedules, and between them all, nineteen different teachers to follow. Between school activities, band and sports practices, church, and birthday parties, I am constantly pulled in a million directions. I'm working outside the home and volunteering in ways that require more time and brain power than ever before. Even with friends helping with car pool or bringing dinner over, I often feel exhausted and as if I'm always reacting to something unexpected that has happened.

Meanwhile, up in space, Drew's life is tight and regimented. From the moment the crew wakes up in the morning, every hour is accounted for in five-minute increments. The crew works a twelve-hour day, bookended by meals and personal time. The biggest block of free time Drew has is before his sleep time begins, which is also tightly scheduled. The best—and really only—time for him to call home is around 9 p.m. before he heads to bed an hour later. Sounds great, except the station follows Greenwich Mean Time, which is either five or six hours ahead of Texas, depending on whether we're on daylight saving time. That means that his calls always fall at the worst time of the day for me—the dreaded 4 to 5 p.m. window.

My cell phone vibrates on the kitchen counter. I wipe my hands on a towel and flip it over my shoulder as I glance at my phone to see who it is.

"Drew on Space Station" scrolls across the screen while the cheerful ringtone urges me to hurry up and tap Accept. This isn't a great time to talk, but you can't exactly not answer a call from space.

"Hey! What are you doing?" he asks while orbiting the Earth.

"Just got back from picking Daniel up from swim practice, so I'm getting started on dinner. Kids are working on homework." I glance over at the kitchen table, where Sophia is waving at me, pointing at her worksheet and mouthing, "Help!"

I desperately want to talk to Drew, to hear what's going on with the crew and tell him about my day, but this is a terrible time. I need to drop Amelia off at small group in ninety minutes, and dinner is barely started. I hold up a finger to Sophia, letting her know I'll be right back. Once in the bedroom, I can close the door and steal a few precious minutes.

"I have so many things I need to tell you, that I want to talk with you about, but this day is crazy," I tell Drew.

"What's going on?"

Where do I begin? The parenting issues in this season are so heavy and pile up so quickly. Lying, teenage heartbreak, bullying, friendship disappointments, GPAs, adolescent hormones, body image, college prep. We've been talking on the phone every day since Drew left, but too often our conversations are just passing info exchanges, inconveniently timed around too many listening ears for a quality, in-depth connection.

"Is there any way you can call later?" I ask. "Maybe thirty minutes? I can get things on track here and then break away." I hear something heavy drop on the kitchen floor. It sounds wet.

"Okay," he says. "But I have only another hour until I have to go to bed. We'll have to be quick."

This time difference is killing me. For about the first month, we make it work. I lock myself in the bedroom while the kids roam around the house, unsupervised and hungry until we hang up and I start parenting again. But then school starts, and we are forced to face the harsh reality that we have eight more months of this bad timing ahead of us. Clearly the communication patterns we used a decade ago during deployment are not going to work now. It's time to get creative.

Drew and I like to talk every day, and there's no shortage of news to share. But we don't have hours to do a deep dive on marital issues or parenting strategies. I feel the pressure of his daily timeline as much as he does. I don't want him hungry or tired or distracted during the workday—the stakes are too high. So we attempt to adapt.

When Drew was in combat, his movements and activities were far less public and often veiled in secrecy. Now, most everything he does in space is available for me to see online and experience virtually. I can drop into televised interviews, scroll through pictures on social media, and watch uploaded videos of Drew doing everything from mind-blowing science experiments to brushing his teeth. By reading or viewing enough of these pieces, I can gain what feels like a sense of intimacy. But it isn't real. It is just space news, content produced to inform and entertain. I find great value in it, but not for deepening connection.

Drew and I start using email like text, shooting each other quick messages throughout the day. Brief updates, simple questions, and pictures sent back and forth make us feel more connected. We give each other permission to say "This isn't a great day for a phone call" and not take it personally. If there's something big we need to talk about, we set the expectation for a serious call so I can plan ahead and adjust the evening routine to make more time.

But more importantly, we realize that I cannot be Drew's sole meaningful connection to home in the way I was when he was deployed. In the same way, I have to accept that he cannot fully meet my need for companionship during this season. We will need to grow and layer our circles of connection in a more intentional way than in the past.

Drew starts calling friends and family regularly, often on their birthdays or other big occasions, or simply when I don't have time to talk. The magic words "Hi! This is Drew calling from the space station!" create a frenzy of excitement and joy from others that I simply can't muster on a daily basis. Every single person he calls is thrilled to hear from him, delighted to catch him up on what's going on in their life. It's a huge morale boost for him, and a huge burden lifted off me. I want Drew to know that he is loved and missed every day and that people all over the globe are tracking what he is doing. We are all rooting for and praying for him. I want him to be encouraged by an army of cheerleaders, and the reality is that with all the balls I need to keep in the air, some days that just won't be me. But our people are there, ready and wanting to connect with him.

Back on Earth, I don't need a cheerleader, I need a companion. My days are full, and often it feels like my body is moving faster than my brain. But in the evenings, when the kids are finally in bed and the house is quiet, my brain has a chance to catch up.

"You're not going to believe what I heard today . . ."
"I saw this hilarious meme today . . ."
"They opened that new restaurant down the street today . . ."
"My knee started hurting today . . ."
"Does this mole look different today . . . ?"
"The car made a weird noise today . . ."

These are the kinds of random thoughts Drew and I would discuss while getting ready for bed if Drew were home. One of us would toss one out while brushing our teeth before we jumped to the next, sharing the kind of scraps not worthy of entire conversations but significant enough to feel we had to get them out of our heads before the end of the day. As we'd lie down in bed and turn off the light, one of us would inevitably roll over with one more thing to say before we fell asleep.

These are the connections I miss most while Drew is gone. The stray thoughts that bubble up late at night have no ear to land in. I know that by the time I finish dinner, Drew is already zipped into his sleeping bag in his phone booth–size crew quarters, strapped to the wall so he doesn't float away. A few hours later in the dark, my brain is overflowing, and I feel isolated and alone with no one to talk to. I want to sit with another adult in comfortable silence or share my scattered thoughts. If I have something urgent or profound to say, there are plenty of people I could call. My parents and many friends and family members would love to hear from me. But if I called, they'd expect a conversation, and that's not what I need. I'm craving connection, but in a casual, single thought kind of way that expects to give or receive nothing more. Without this type of connection, I'm lonely.

At first, I try to fill the space in my mental conversations by reading books, listening to music, or binge-watching Netflix late into the night. In the end, it doesn't matter how late I stay up, when I lie in bed, it's still just me alone with the thoughts I had no one to tell that day.

"This isn't working," I say to myself one night. "Oh great. Now you're talking to yourself. We definitely need to figure this out."

The next day while getting ready for work, I try something new. I record a video message for my friend using the Marco Polo app. I'm delighted when she sends one back while I am eating breakfast. I send her another after the kids go to bed, telling her what I did that day. She responds with her own thoughts. I listen to it while I brush my teeth. I record one more with a few additional random observations and rambling sentences. When I go to bed that night, my brain is empty for the first time in a while.

The next night I text a friend who I know is watching the same PBS Masterpiece special I am.

"This actor playing the bad guy. I know him from another show. What's he from?"

"Yes! Who is that guy?" she texts right back.

"I'll look him up," I write. We text our jokes and commentary back and forth during the rest of the show, and it almost feels like we're watching it together. It's a different kind of companionship, but it's working. I don't feel so alone anymore.

* * *

Learning how to stay connected in new ways while Drew was in space was a difficult lesson for us, and one a lot of people struggled to learn during the pandemic. Finding connection when life is hard and you feel alone can seem complicated or almost impossible. It's easy to get frustrated and simply give up. When a person you've come to depend on is no longer able to fill your needs in the same way, you may feel disappointed or even betrayed. But we are not meant to be alone or to connect with only one person. God desires that we live in community. That is why we must continue to reach out and form bonds with others, even when crazy events like launches into space or worldwide pandemics turn everything we've ever known about how to "do" relationships upside down. As the apostle Paul told the church, "Encourage one another and build each other up" (1 Thessalonians 5:11).

The Greek word for "build" in this verse usually applies to the physical building of houses, but Paul often used it to suggest people lifting each other up. Like constructing a house, building connections can be hard work, and no two houses—or relationships—are exactly alike. Connections morph and evolve over time, changing to meet our unique circumstances and personalities. But in our deepest connections, we build upon one another, always seeking a sense of belonging and a richer understanding of the other person.

✳ ✳ ✳

When Drew was overseas, I knew he was doing dangerous things. I knew he was experiencing things I could never fully comprehend because I wasn't there. I gleaned enough from our phone calls and video sessions to grasp the fact that these months spent in combat would be some of the worst, and best, of his life. Civilians often are surprised to learn that not all days in a combat zone are full of terror and death, that just as many are full of life, laughter, and extreme boredom. There's a common misconception that all deployed soldiers are desperately counting the days until they come home and that they never want to deploy again. In our military community at least, that couldn't have been further from the truth. While Drew certainly looked forward to coming home, his fellow soldiers were his brothers. The bond of knowing that you will live or die together and that, no matter what, you will never leave one another's side, is incredibly powerful.

There's an entry in Drew's combat journal that has always stuck with me. A fellow warrior and friend had been mortally wounded and was under Drew's care in a field hospital. He was too unstable to transport. Drew wrote that he told the rest of his team the truth: He believed that, given the choice between dying midflight on the way to a bigger medical facility or dying right there, surrounded by his friends, the man would unquestionably choose the latter. So they stayed there, with him until the end. Together as a team, they experienced horrible, scary things. But they also protected each other, cared for each other, celebrated together, ate together, watched movies together, worked out together, and enjoyed life together. They became a brotherhood, united in purpose and forged in fire. It's an experience that cannot be replicated in peacetime or in the comfort of home. That deployment season becomes a touchpoint in life, for good or bad, and one that many seek to experience repeatedly because for them, the good far outweighs the bad.

Some of us left behind struggle to understand the dichotomy between the hardship of service and the enjoyment of camaraderie among soldiers. As spouses, we want to understand what our soldiers experienced, but they aren't sure even how to process what they went through. When well-intentioned family members ask, "So how was the war?" and expect a meaningful answer, we shake our heads. If I've learned anything, it's that the answer to that common question is far from simple. It was good and bad. It was terrible and it was wonderful. And as much as I wanted to fully share in Drew's experience, that was impossible. I wasn't there to live through it, just as it was impossible for him to fully understand what it was like back home because he wasn't there either. So in our long-distance conversations, we shared the news and said what we could, but we both knew we were just scratching the surface.

I'd attended enough spouse support meetings to know the dangers of pushing him too hard to talk about what deployment life was like when his unit returned home. The stress of an abrupt return to family is well documented by military psychologists. To be in a combat zone one day, then back home mowing the lawn the next, is not an easy transition. Add a nagging spouse, difficult children, tight finances, or any other number of problematic variables, and you have a recipe for anger, bitterness, emotional withdrawal, divorce, alcohol or spousal abuse, or worse. Wise spouses tread carefully, waiting for opportunities to ask well-timed questions about those long months away.

After returning home, Drew suggested I read his journals. "It will probably take you a while. These aren't journal entries full of feelings and flowery descriptions, but I think you might be interested to learn more about what I was doing."

"Yes, of course I am! I'll start right away," I said with outward enthusiasm. But inside, I wasn't so sure. What if I learned things I didn't want to know? About Drew? About his unit? About the harsh realities of combat and this dangerous life we'd chosen? When it came to war, perhaps ignorance was bliss. Yet my curiosity and desire to connect with Drew carried me through page after page. His brief but informative entries gave me a window into his life that I could otherwise never have seen.

I smiled over entries about birthday celebrations and meaningful interactions with locals. I was amazed and humbled when I read about the incredible courage these men showed in the face of danger. And I cried, clutching my stomach, as I read about the terrible deaths of friends and comrades, described in far more gritty detail than the sterile descriptions shared on the news. But more than anything, his words gave me a place to start a conversation, a way to gently step into a moment in time with curiosity. After reading an interesting, funny, or heartbreaking entry, I'd come to Drew, journal in hand.

"You had a cake on your birthday? Who bought it for you? Where did they get it?"

"I didn't know your interpreter was with you in the vehicle. Did they go with you on every mission?"

"I just read about what happened in early April. Can you tell me more about that? It sounds like it was really hard on everyone."

Though I wasn't in combat with him and we'd lived parallel but separate lives for that season, these conversations allowed us to build bridges across those gaps. They gave me a level of understanding and compassion I couldn't have found otherwise. They helped us connect on a deeper level again. For while we weren't able to share the events themselves, we could share the experience of telling our stories to each other, which was the next best thing.

* * *

The irony that Drew left the space station, where he lived in a small, isolated space with five professional crewmates, only to come home and live in a small, isolated space with five family crewmates (thanks to COVID-19) is not lost on us. Pre-pandemic, a return from space is a lot like a return from a deployment. In space one day, home the next—a relatively abrupt transition back to home life, or in the case of an astronaut, Earth life. The pandemic changes almost every aspect of Drew's return, eliminating the usual interactions with friends, family, and fellow astronauts that help smooth the shift back to gravity and normal family routines. Instead, as a family, we are isolated in the crew quarantine facility at Johnson Space Center first. Then later we hunker down together at home. With most media appearances and all but essential medical testing and physical therapy sessions canceled, Drew and I are together for more hours in the day than we have been in years.

"We cannot forget to write in our journals about the landing experience and this new normal," Drew reminds me less than twenty-four hours after landing back on Earth. "There are so many details I want to remember, and I know I need to get them down before I forget. But I don't think I can type that much right now. What would you think about doing an audio recording instead?" he asks.

I'm not nearly as dedicated a journal writer as Drew is, so this sounds like a great suggestion to me. "Absolutely. I have a good microphone I can plug into my laptop. When do you want to start?"

"How about tomorrow night? There's not much to do while we're stuck here in the quarantine facility anyway."

The next day we put the kids in front of a movie and set up my laptop on a table in the conference room.

"It's April 22; it's a Wednesday," our first audio recording begins. "We're in the astronaut quarantine facility at Johnson Space Center, and we're reflecting back on the last couple of days."

"Okay, so let's talk about the day of landing for the crew on the station. What does that morning look like when you get up?" I ask.

"Well, it was kind of just a normal workday in some regards." *A normal workday? The day you are returning to Earth? How is that possible? It wasn't even normal for me!*

As Drew speaks about that day, I am reminded of how little I really knew about his experience. Because Drew's nine-month mission extended longer than the typical six months, he returned to Earth with a different two-person crew than the one he launched with, something that does not happen often. In fact, his launch crewmates, Aleksandr and Luca, had returned to Earth over two months earlier. His landing crew, NASA classmate Jessica Meir and Russian commander Oleg Skripochka, had a different dynamic and way of doing things than his launch crew, making the experience even more unique.

"Did you have time to reflect?" I ask. "Was there a moment when you took one last look around your crew quarters and said to yourself, *I am now leaving my crew quarters for the last time, or I am leaving the ISS for the last time, so I want to take one last look*? Or is that not something that happened?"

"Not really," he answers. He explains that the astronauts' schedule that day included an extra rest period to help their bodies begin the time adjustment for Earth. "Because of that, it felt like we had a lot of extra time to get things done, and then the day accelerated in that last hour. And then all of a sudden, it's time to go and you're back at the docking port. The camera's on, you're waving goodbye, and you know that you're live on the internet with everyone watching. After that we climbed in and closed the hatch."

Drew's description of his final day fascinates me because when the live coverage began, most of what he's telling me about had already happened. I want to know every detail, so I ask lots of questions.

"What were you saying to each other before you climbed back into the Soyuz?"

"Who decided you would all wear the same pants?"

"Did you bring any snacks with you?"

Drew isn't always a smooth storyteller, but this time it's easy for him because we're following the story down its actual timeline.

"Once we got in and they closed the hatch, we started doing vehicle leak checks. But someone had to immediately start to put their suit on. Jessica was first because she sat in the left seat. So Oleg got her suited up, and I just stayed out of the way. Then it was my turn because I was in the right seat. Oleg, as the commander sitting in the middle, suited up last. We did stash a couple of snacks in there. I had a Snickers bar, just like I did before every EVA. So I ate that really quick and had a drink. Once we were done, we just put the trash up in the habitation module, which burned up on reentry."

As he talks though the details of strapping in and completing their suit pressure checks, I feel like I'm in the Soyuz with him. The capsule undocks from the station with a muffled thud, its heavy latches springing open so the Soyuz can back away like a car slowly pulling out of a tight parking space. As it floats away, the stubby, winglike solar arrays on the sides of the spacecraft harness the power of the sun to get the vehicle back to Earth.

Then it's my turn to talk about what the kids and I did that day. Families of US astronauts stay in Texas during Soyuz landings because while the capsule lands back on Earth in Kazakhstan, the crew is flown back to the States only about twenty-four hours after hitting the ground. We watch the crew get back into their Soyuz vehicle and undock from the space station from the comfort of our own living rooms. Some families make a party of it and invite over dozens of friends to celebrate, but with full quarantine restrictions in place for us, the kids and I watched the undocking alone.

"We spent the day killing time," I tell Drew. "Anything to make the day go by faster. I went for a run and finished a puzzle. We watched a movie. Friends brought over Mexican food. Like you, I felt like we had all this time to kill, then suddenly we had to hurry to get in the car and drive to Johnson Space Center to watch the landing."

Drew asks me lots of questions.

"Who brought the food over?"

"What movie did you watch?"

"Who was with you at mission control?"

"Tell me more about the kids' reaction when they watched the landing."

I can tell from his face that, in his imagination, he's there with us at mission control, just as I feel I was with him in the capsule. It's not the same as actually being there together, but it's the next best thing.

* * *

Meaningful, life-giving connections are built brick by brick, layer by layer, by people dedicated to encouraging one another as Paul exhorts us to do. Like building a strong house, forging strong connections is hard work. It can be dirty and complex, and sometimes the best ideas don't work out as planned. But if you want to have shelter from the storms of this life, you have to keep building and you cannot do it alone. If you want a house strong enough to last, you bring in a team of specialists, all working together in different ways to create something greater than the sum of their parts.

Don't do life solo. Call in the specialists—your family and friends. Invite them to build with you; hand them a tool. They'll get to work, building you up as you build connections together. Even in the darkest, hardest, most upside-down days, you may be isolated, but you will not be alone.

CHAPTER 5

LET THE GOOD TIMES ROLL

REDISCOVER FUN

About halfway through Drew's space mission, I decide it's time to get rid of the old television we've been hauling around the country for almost two decades. A vacuum tube behemoth, deeper than it is wide, this TV has reached the end of its useful life. I haul it downstairs, no small feat given how heavy and awkwardly square it is. My arms are too tired to take it farther than the garage, so there it sits, forlorn and waiting for a special trash pickup later in the month.

A week later, I am on the phone with my friend Allison when I mention the TV. "I'm getting tired of walking around it every time I need to get to my car, but I guess I don't have a choice. There's not much else I can do with it."

Allison chuckles. "You know, I have an old TV we just took out of my mom's house. Big giant thing with the cathode-ray tube, just like yours. You know what I think we should do . . ."

The idea hits us both at the same time. You can practically see the light bulbs flash above our heads.

"Are you thinking what I'm thinking?" Allison asks.

"Smash them with sledgehammers?"

"Exactly."

A new chain of smash rooms has just opened in our area. Regular people visit these places and pay good money to enter a room full of old electronics, china plates, furniture, glass bottles, and other breakables and shatter everything with the provided baseball bat. (Think of the scene where three frustrated employees take a bat to their fax machine in the 1999 movie *Office Space* and you get the idea.) It's supposed to be a great form of stress relief.

"Saturday, my backyard," Allison says.

"I'm there. And let's video it in slow motion."

That glorious November morning dawns bright and crisp. Dressed in an old pair of army camouflage pants, a pink baseball hat, and light blue yard gloves, I hoist the heavy TV out of the back of my minivan and hobble into the backyard. Allison has already prepped the smash space. A large blue tarp lies across the grass, her old TV ready and waiting in the middle. A sledgehammer, an ax, a baseball bat, and a large crowbar lean against a nearby tree. I lower my TV down next to hers. A friendly neighbor wanders over and announces he's been recruited to be our videographer.

"Great!" Allison says. "Let's get started!" I pick up the ax. Allison grabs the sledgehammer. I put on my safety glasses and assume a Babe Ruth, knock-it-out-of-the-park batter's stance.

"On the count of three," I say. "One . . . two . . . three!"

We both pull back and swing forward, hitting our respective televisions square in the middle of the glass screens at the same time.

Boooom!! The colossal explosion temporarily stuns us, and we stagger a step backward. We turn and look at each other with startled eyes through the thick plastic of our safety glasses. But then the raw thrill of destroying something kicks in, and together we let out an excited whoop.

"That was *awesome!*" A foggy vapor rises up out of both splintered TV screens. We hoot and howl as we continue to attack the televisions. Apparently we are both more stressed than we realized. From the top, from the side, with the baseball bat, with the crowbar—we keep swinging and smashing until all that is left of the televisions is a pile of small glass chunks, plastic bits, and twisted wire.

Breathless, Allison and I rest our weapons on the ground, and our videographer hands back our phones. We watch the footage, snorting as we see the expression of surprise on our faces when the glass shatters on the first blow. In slow motion, it looks even cooler. I am surprised at how much more relaxed I feel, and I can't wait to send this video to Drew on the space station.

A few weeks earlier, he sent me a video that made me laugh harder than I have in a long time. In it, Drew's crewmates zip him into a large cloth storage container, his smiling face sticking out of the corner of the bag while they push him around the station like a floating bag of trash. Seeing these usually very serious astronauts joke around so playfully did my soul some good. Until then, I hadn't realized how important it is for me to know that even in space, Drew has opportunities to laugh and play. I know that often in our daily phone conversations, I dwell too long on the hardest parts of my day, so seeing a video of me laughing and playing will do Drew some good too.

Over the next few days, Allison and I show the video to as many people as humanly possible. We had such a blast smashing those televisions, we expect an equally enthusiastic response from our friends.

Instead, the first question we are asked most often is this: "How did you clean it all up?"

Every time someone asks us this ridiculous question, we are indignant.

"What do you mean, how did we clean it up? It was on a tarp; we picked it all up, put it in the trash, whatever. You're missing the big picture here! We smashed two giant TVs into kibble in the backyard, and that's all you want to know? How did we clean it up? Are you kidding me?"

But that's precisely what they want to know because that's how most of us, as adults, measure fun. Sure, we want to have a good time, but not if it requires too much cleanup. We like fun as long as it's not too loud, too complicated, too hot outside, or too time-consuming. We don't want to get our new sneakers dirty or have to take a shower afterward. If it's not a learning experience, quality family time, or good cardio exercise, then what's the point?

This is the opposite of how we defined fun when we were younger. Making mud pies, dancing in the rain, hiding in the woods, dressing up in costumes, or getting covered in chalk dust, bicycle grease, dead leaves, baking flour, or paint splatter—that was our definition of play and recreation. I remember an event at a high school church camp where we set up a giant slip-and-slide down a big hill, but instead of using water to coast down it, we used vanilla pudding. I can't imagine how much pudding the camp kitchen staff had to provide—I can only guess it was buckets and buckets of the stuff. All I know is that everyone had a blast. I didn't give a second thought to what that pudding would do to my shoes, shorts, or shirt, or how I'd have to wash the pudding out of my hair later. Sliding down that big hill on a giant plastic sheet covered in pudding remains one of the highlights of that summer. Twenty-five years later, I still remember it fondly. As kids, we lived for the novelty and whimsy of life and wandered off in search of it every day with little regard for anything else.

What happens to us as we age? At what point do we start caring more about the cleanup than the fun itself? When did amusement change from part of our fundamental worldview to something that happens only on special occasions, when we can gather up enough people to make it worth our while and find enough time to schedule it in between having our teeth cleaned and our oil changed? As adults, we define fun as going to dinner, a movie, or a ball game. Those are all great, but they aren't whimsical. They aren't messy or risky. There's no spontaneity. There's no skill or learning something new involved. It's as if we outgrow fun—at least the way we defined it when we were young.

Some might argue that this is just part of growing up; that as we get older, we redefine "fun" based on what's important to us in that stage of life. But I don't think it has anything to do with our biological age. I think many of us decide as adults that safety, stability, and continuity are the essentials in life and that we must sacrifice whimsy to have them. I think we determine that our fear of getting hurt or looking silly should override our willingness to be spontaneous or try something new. For some people, this switch happens when they get that first big promotion, have their first serious relationship, or get married. For some, it's when they buy a house or get a dog. For many women like me, it's when they become moms. That's when, in my mind, I became a real adult. While still lying in my hospital bed recovering from the delivery, I felt I had no choice but to put childish things behind me and step fully into this new season of parenthood, a time of seriousness focused on keeping this helpless baby alive. To be a good mom, I thought, I had to redefine myself and rearrange my priorities. In the shuffle, I left whimsy—and a little piece of myself—behind.

✳ ✳ ✳

Here are some typical conversations Drew and I shared between 1998 and 2003 when fun and whimsy were still fundamental to how I lived my life:

1998 Me: "I have two free periods in my class schedule, so I'm going to sign up for a massage class and scuba diving lessons."

Drew: "Sounds cool. But what do those classes have to do with your economics degree?"

Me: "Absolutely nothing. But I'll learn how to give great back rubs, and next summer we can scuba dive together. Maybe someday we can book a trip to Hawaii!"

(Spoiler: I did not learn how to give great back rubs, at least according to Drew.)

1999 Me: "I got a job today at the Smithsonian Air and Space Museum! I'm going to give demonstrations about airplanes, crack a whip to explain sonic booms, and organize paper airplane contests."

Drew: "Sounds cool. But don't you already have a job with that investment firm?"

Me: "I'll do both! And I get a 20 percent discount in the gift shop! Guess where I'm getting everyone's Christmas presents?"

(Spoiler: Drew got freeze-dried "astronaut" ice cream for Christmas that year.)

2000 Me: "While you're away at training, I'm going to learn American Sign Language through night classes at the local community college!"

Drew: "Sounds cool. But what does that have to do with your real job as a business consultant?"

Me: "Absolutely nothing. But I can't wait to learn how to tell a joke using just my hands!"

(Spoiler: I don't remember much, but I do remember that the sign for "grandma" and "vomit" are very similar, so don't get them confused.)

2001 Me: "I'm going to apply to be a contestant on that new reality TV game show, *The Mole.*"

Drew: "Sounds cool. Do you really think they'll pick you?"

Me: "Who knows? But I've already talked to your brother, and he's coming down this weekend to help me shoot and edit a crazy audition video. I can't wait!"

(Spoiler: Unbelievably, they didn't pick me. I'm still 100 percent convinced I would have been awesomely sneaky on that show and won the entire thing.)

2002 Me: "Let's go cross-country skiing tomorrow."

Drew: "Sounds cool. But neither of us actually knows how to cross-country ski."

Me: "I'm sure we'll figure it out. How hard can it be?"

(Spoiler: It was hard. Like really hard. And I was sore for a week afterward.)

2003 Me: "I'm so tired. This baby is so fussy. I don't know what to do."

Drew: "Do you want to go out and do something? Maybe getting out of the house would help."

Me: "It's too hard to leave the house with a baby. Have you

seen the mega-size diaper bag I haul around? Plus, the baby needs to take a nap, so I can't go anywhere. Life is too hard to do *anything*." I lie on the floor and cry.

(Spoiler: This was pretty much my first six months as a mom. Super fun.)

* * *

For those who just had their first baby last week, what I'm about to tell you may come as shocking news. Looking back on my almost two decades as a mom, I can see that in certain seasons—sometimes spanning months, sometimes lasting years—I have lost myself. Anyone who has been a "responsible adult" for longer than a week knows what I'm talking about. For reasons outside of your control, you have to put your own hopes, desires, or expectations on hold because your life must revolve around something or someone else for a time. Whether it's because of a new baby or your husband's career or kids' sports or your teenagers' schedules or aging parents—whatever it is, you feel as if you have no choice but to put yourself aside to keep this house of popsicle sticks standing. It's basic survival, plain and simple. When the going gets tough, the "responsible adult" buckles down and leaves herself behind in order to get everyone else safely to tomorrow.

This isn't a phenomenon exclusive to motherhood. Those same uncontrollable life forces affect men and women who are married, unmarried, with kids, without kids, just starting work, professionals in their prime, or long-time retirees. No matter your status or lifestyle variables, there's one big common human denominator. It doesn't take much for most of us to be knocked off balance and forced into survival mode.

For me, the first thing I throw overboard when life feels full or complex is fun. I shift into adult survival mode and hyperfocus on feeding, clothing, protecting, and guiding everyone in my inner circle. Fun Proactive-Me moves out and reactionary Survival-Me moves in. I keep everything humming, but I lose my spontaneity, my thirst for adventure, and my desire to learn and try new things. Instead, I become an expert in making my day-to-day life easier and as predictable as possible—cleaning the house, shopping for groceries, making dinner, doing laundry. Rinse and repeat. And repeat. And repeat. Over time, my sparkle dims, dulled by the monotonous routines of life.

Survival-Me has no time for fun. That's for those lucky children whose mom cares enough to schedule fun for them between nap time and twenty minutes of daily reading. To smooth over tough days for my family, Survival-Me looks for ways to make my children happy with no regard for myself. Art classes, swim lessons, summer camp, music lessons, family vacations, new toys, free-time activities—Survival-Me filters everything through the lens of what is best for the children. Does this activity have educational value? Will the kids learn a new skill or build new social connections? Will it teach them to be brave? Will it make them laugh? How different my schedule and my life would be if I asked those same questions about how I spend my own time. Our culture tells us moms aren't supposed to care about exploring new places, making new friends, learning new skills, or having their own adventures. Moms should have outgrown those childish ideas of fun long ago. If you have time to think about those things— or even worse, fit some of them in your schedule—then you clearly aren't "momming" hard enough. Survival-Me knows that moms are supposed to focus on safety, education, balanced nutrition, and good hygiene. Fun and whimsy are extravagant extras, bonuses only for those who finish their chores. And as all responsible adults know, there's always one more chore to be done.

Everyone has survival seasons. That's to be expected when you live in a broken world as we do. But if we stay hunkered down too long, our life can become like a thick, dark swamp—stagnant, scary, dismal, and hard to escape. What nudges me out of my colorless seasons is remembering the truth that God wasn't calling me to become a martyr when he made me a mother, in the same way he doesn't call people to put aside who they are when they get a promotion, get married, buy a house, or adopt a dog. He calls us to an abundant life, full of possibilities for good things, no matter what stage of life we are in or how long and hard our days may feel. We may be responsible adults, but God still wants us to have fun and enjoy the many blessings of his incredible creation and our diverse creativity. When Jesus told his followers, "I have come that they may have life, and have it to the full" (John 10:10), I think he would include not only the changed hearts and new life he offers in himself but also full enjoyment of this dazzling world he created and full embrace of the unique creativity he planted in every soul.

If I believe what Jesus said is true, how am I living that out? My children are watching me, every moment of every day, to see what it means to live a full life. Just because I'm in a challenging season does not mean I should be any less myself. God made me an adventure seeker, a lifelong learner, a risk-taker, and a woman who laughs easily. Switching to autopilot may make life easier today, but I'll pay for it tomorrow with interest. If I don't feed my soul, if I don't remember to laugh and have fun, I am not living a full life. I'm just surviving day to day. Every moment may not be rainbows and unicorns, but that's no excuse to allow Survival-Me to threaten a hostile takeover.

In hard times, we must pursue fun even more intentionally. When we exercise the childlike part of ourselves that seeks out novelty, gets dirty, and smiles often, we readjust our priorities and find ourselves again. It's important that our career, housework, finances, volunteering, and even motherhood take a back seat every so often. It's good for us to get a change in perspective and give those potential idols a kick in the pants once in a while.

Life was stressful when Drew was in space. Single parenting, whether permanently or temporarily, is hard work. There wasn't a day that went by when Survival-Me didn't lean into my ear and whisper, *The house is looking pretty messy. How about you put your book down and let me take over so we can get some real work done? You'll feel better after we knock a few things off the to-do list.*

Often I'd listen to her, and we'd crank through that list as only a serious, all-business Survival-Me can. And as I stood in the middle of my clean house, I felt great. After all, I'm also a person who sometimes makes the first item on my to-do list "make a to-do list" so I can have the satisfaction of checking one task off right away. But if I let Survival-Me stay in charge for too long, I became restless. I realized that once again, by allowing Survival-Me to move in and build a permanent bunker, I traded a bit of myself—my carefree, whimsical, adventurous, fun-loving self—for the temporary high of a clean house. Because I allowed my priorities to reshuffle, my kids saw a woman more interested in getting work done than in reading her favorite book, taking a bike ride, playing a game, or cuddling on the couch. You can say to your child, "I'd love to sit and talk with you, but there's laundry to do," only so many times before you have to decide that enough is enough. Laundry at the expense of connection is not a full life. Checking items off to-do lists at the expense of laughter does not lead to a full life. Merely surviving is not a full life. The laundry will eventually get done. The dishwasher will eventually get emptied. The emails will eventually be responded to. Part of being a responsible adult should be prioritizing having fun.

Stop hustling. Take a break. Do something that feeds your soul and makes you smile. Let's shake off the mental cobwebs and stretch our grown-adult muscles. Let's think back to that hobby we used to love doing and throw ourselves back into it. Let's reminisce about that childhood dream we had to be something, do something, or try something. Be a ballerina, learn to fly a plane, try every Mexican restaurant in town. Pick a dream and then go do it. If not now, when?

* * *

It has been a long week. Every day feels like a slog, and I've let autopilot take over. Get up. Eat breakfast. Get kids out the door. Go to work. Come home. Pick up kids. Help with homework. Make dinner. Repeat until your brain feels numb.

Tap. Tap.

A light knock interrupts me while I'm mindlessly wiping the kitchen counter. As I approach the front door, I can see the retreating figure of someone walking down the sidewalk, hands full of flyers, one of which they have just stuck in my front door handle. A flash of annoyance flares through me. I assume it is the usual advertisement for a local restaurant or a lawn service. I jerk the door open, and a fluorescent-green paper flutters to the ground. As I bend to pick it up, the clip art of a roller skate in the upper right corner catches my eye. Now, this is something new—roller-skating classes at our local rink. I scan the words on the sheet.

Join us every Saturday for roller-skating lessons!
All ages welcome!
One lesson or six-week session packages available.
Call to reserve your spot today!

In a flash, it's 1986. I'm in third grade and walking into one of my favorite places on Earth, the Wal-Lex roller rink. The Wal-Lex, short for Waltham-Lexington, the two towns the rink straddles, is an eight-year-old kid's fantasy. For me, everything about the place is fantastic and mysterious, and for everyone in my elementary school, this is the place to have a birthday party. The building is enormous, at least from my 4'6" perspective, and as I enter through the main doors, I pass a small alcove filled with the beeps of classic arcade games, barely audible over the pulsating Top 40 music filling the massive space. I feel the pull of the shiny pinball machines' blinking lights, but I walk on to reach the strange Dutch half-door set into the wall. A gray-haired woman beckons me to the counter, gesturing for me to put my scuffed sneakers on the worn wooden surface.

She tilts her head as if to share a dark secret with me. As I lean forward, she hisses, "What size?"

"Four," I whisper as she snatches my shoes and turns to complete her secret, magic swap. I stand up on my tiptoes and peer over the top of the door. Inside, the room is a cave of wonders, filled with racks and racks of brown skates. The shelves seem to reach up to the ceiling and recede back for miles. *Where is she taking my shoes? How does she know where to put them? And how will she ever find them again?*

The old woman shuffles back and drops my skates on the counter, the orange wheels banging together, a giant red number four on the back of each skate, letting everyone know exactly how big my feet are. I grab them by the laces and sink to the floor next to the door, shoving my feet in and quickly lacing them up so I don't miss another second of fun.

Just a few steps behind me, the expansive parquet floor begins, surrounded by a metal railing covered in strips of old carpet, perfect for little hands to grip onto. I stumble-step toward the rink and begin pulling myself around the edge. I'm not a bad skater, but I'm not great, either. If I start to struggle, I can head to the edge at any time and use the railing to steady myself. It runs almost the entire circumference of the rink, except for the section on the far side where a black painted stage looms over the brightly lit floor. The stage is never in use during the birthday parties I attend on early Saturday afternoons, but its existence hints that after dark, something incredible must happen here. Why else would they hang colored spotlights and glittering disco balls from the ceiling? In my prepubescent mind's eye, I can imagine the fantastic parties teenagers must attend here on Friday nights. I picture them gliding across the floor as lights flash against the tiny mirrors on the disco balls, sending a cascade of artificial fireflies around the room. Live rock music from the stage serenades young lovers, hands locked together for a couples-only skate. This is an eight-year-old's romantic fantasy. For now, an afternoon zipping around the floor with my friends, overhead lights blazing, will have to do.

A little boy in the middle of the traffic flow stumbles and sprawls on the floor, which is the roller-skating equivalent of a car crash in the middle of a multilane highway. If he doesn't get up quickly, there'll be a NASCAR-level pileup on the floor in a matter of seconds. From the corner of my eye, I see a flash of black-and-white stripes zip by as the cavalry arrives, effortlessly hooking the little boy's arm and lifting him back to his feet. As I glide by, I gaze up at the rescuer, one of the teenage skate referees who roam the rink in endless circles, snatching up tumbling children and reminding us to be careful and follow traffic. To my friends and me, they are roller-skating gods. Whether racing forward, backward, twisting, turning, bending, or spinning—their skate confidence is incredible. We want to know them, touch them, be them. To have that level of skating ability is too impossible to imagine. So we watch and try to copy them, grabbing at the carpet-covered railing when our skates fly out from underneath us.

Now, years later, I stare at this electric-green flyer with the roller skate clip art. Yes. This.

I pick up the phone and call the number on the bottom of the page. A friendly voice answers.

"Hello!" I say, "I received your flyer on my door today, and I have a few questions. It says all ages. Is that really true, or is this just for kids?"

"Oh yes," the man says, "all ages! We've got lots of adults, even a grandpa who comes with his granddaughter."

A grandpa? I think, imaging my frail, old grandfather who played the accordion and sent me five dollars on my birthday every year. I know I must at least be a better skater than someone's grandpa.

"Okay," I say. "My daughters and I will be there on Saturday. I'd like to register four people: one adult and three kids." Daniel has another commitment on Saturdays, or he'd be joining us too.

When the kids walk in after school, I'm so excited I can hardly contain myself.

"We're going to take roller-skating lessons!" I tell the girls.

"Roller-skating?" Amelia asks with the same tone she'd use if I just told her we were going to shave our heads.

"Roller-skating!" Sophia and Gabriella exclaim in disbelief. They've got skates in the garage that they use to toddle up and down the sidewalk, and they still get invited to the occasional birthday party at the roller rink.

"Yes! We're all going to take lessons together. It's going to be amazing." In my mind, I'm already wearing a referee's shirt and skating backward, effortlessly picking kids up by the elbows before their butts even hit the ground. Those teenagers did it. How hard could it be?

Saturday morning, we pull into the roller rink parking lot a few minutes later than I intended. I'd had a hard time figuring out what a forty-year-old woman should wear to roller-skating lessons. If I went in full athletic gear, I might look like I'm trying too hard. I'm realistic enough to know I may fall a few times today, so I didn't want to wear clothes that are too nice to get dirty. I finally settled on jeans and a long-sleeve T-shirt. I wonder what all the other adult students will be wearing.

We walk in the door, sign in, and get our skates. Plenty of other adults are milling about, helping their kids lace up the stiff leather skates. A few loiter near the edge of the floor, but most seem more interested in their phones than getting ready for class. I'm sure they'll put their skates on when they realize the class is about to start.

"Good morning, everyone!" A man's chipper voice cuts through the upbeat music playing over the loudspeakers. "Lots of new faces today! That's great! If this is your first lesson, we'll have you over here with the beginner group. Gold, silver, and bronze groups can spread out in your usual places. Let's get rolling!"

The girls and I stand up and start skating toward the area for beginners. A dozen kids start moving that way too. As they roll away, their parents peel off and settle into seats along the far side of the rink. We reach the beginner area, and I awkwardly attempt to turn around without falling on my behind—and that's when it hits me. I'm the only adult in this class. Even worse, I'm one of only three adults (other than the instructors) wearing skates in this entire rink. Where are all the other adults they promised me?

As the friendly female instructor, who seems to be dressed more for Roller Derby than beginner skating, starts us on some easy drills, I size up the other adult students. I can see the grandpa I heard about over the phone. He is over in the gold group. It's safe to say he's nothing like I imagined. A big, robust man, he's wearing his own professional-quality skates, like most of the students in the gold group. They're looping a figure eight around their side of the rink, effortlessly switching from one foot to the other, forward, then backward. His granddaughter skates behind him, equally skilled.

Over in the silver group, a mom who looks about my age glides across the floor. I watch her for a few minutes out of the corner of my eye as I skate back and forth, shifting my weight and bending at the knees as instructed. She's not *that* much better than me, I think. Then she stops and changes direction with a move I know would have me on my butt in a split second. Scratch that; she's way better than me.

With all those hours at the Wal-Lex, I've got some moderate, albeit dusty, skating skills. You can't attend a dozen roller-skating parties a year for a decade without picking up an adequate level of competence. Compared to my dozen or so classmates, most under the age of ten, I'm a superstar. I can only imagine what the moms sitting on the side of the rink think as they watch me roll back and forth with their first graders. As I line up for our next drill, I feel a soft little hand slide into mine. It's one of my classmates from the beginner group, a girl around the age of seven. She looks up at me with big, beautiful brown eyes and says, "I have to go to the bathroom."

"Uh, okay. It's right over there. Why don't you tell your mom you need some help." This girl is clearly as confused about me being in this class as her parents probably are. My girls are giggling behind me as I help the little girl get to the side of the rink.

The adorable instructor in the tiny Roller Derby skirt and low-slung skates glides over. "So, it looks like you've skated before!"

"Well, I am forty years old" is what I want to say. Instead, I decide to be straight with her. "Yeah, I used to skate a lot as a kid. I'm here with my girls as a fun thing to do together. They said there would be more adults."

She chuckles. "Well, you and your girls are all good enough that next class, you can move up to the bronze group. In the meantime, let me get you working on a skill we call Shoot the Duck. You're going to get a little speed, then drop your butt down to sit on one skate while you keep the other leg straight and lift it off the ground and point it out in front of you."

Um, what? For the past thirty minutes, we've been slowly skating back and forth, just shifting weight from one foot to the other and practicing stopping. The most challenging skills we've worked on to this point are making little hops and lifting one foot off the ground. This new move feels like a massive escalation in difficulty. I'm pretty sure I've seen Olympic figure skaters do something similar in competition. *There's no way . . .*

"You mean like this?" Amelia pushes off, drops her butt, and holds her leg out in front of her. Sophia follows close behind with near-perfect form.

"Exactly!" the instructor says as she skates off, her tiny skirt fluttering behind her. "I'll leave you to it."

The girls turn and look at me expectantly. I can't get my butt that far down when I'm standing still while wearing sneakers, let alone moving across the floor on roller skates. But I can hear my own words coming back to haunt me.

It's exciting to try new things.

Who cares what other people think?

What's the worst that could happen?

Just do your best.

It will be fun being together.

The four of us spend the rest of the class working on Shoot the

Duck. I get as low as I can, but compared to the girls, I'm barely bending over. The move is so hard that I have to focus, and for the last few minutes of class, I almost forget about the other, non-skating adults sitting around the rink with nothing to do but stare. At the end of class, they crank the pop music back up for free skate practice time. We start getting a little cocky.

"Let's make some videos to send to Daddy."

We take turns gliding by the camera, showing off the basic moves we learned that morning.

"Okay, time for Shoot the Duck!" I say.

All three girls roll by, butt down, leg out, amazingly comfortable after just one lesson.

"Your turn!" Sophia skates over and takes my phone, ready to record.

I glide over to the edge of the rink, turn, push off to pick up some speed, and drop my backside as low as it will go. But as I start to pull my leg forward, I lose my balance and sit back too far. My front leg flies up in the air as my butt lands hard on my skate beneath me. I bounce off the wheels and hit the floor with all the grace of a sack of potatoes falling out of the back of an 18-wheeler. *Thud.* This is what it must feel like to break a hip. I've fallen and I can't get up. I moan as I roll over onto all fours and see the girls laughing hysterically, still filming. I crawl to the side and try not to make eye contact with anyone in the room.

But as they turn the phone around and show me the video, I can't help but laugh too. I look ridiculous. My fall is spectacularly uncoordinated, legs flying, arms braced toward the floor, doing exactly what they told us *not* to do, while flocks of little kids stream by me. It's an objective fact; my fall is hilariously painful to both my body and my pride. In that moment, the skating fantasy of my eight-year-old self dies. I'm never going to be as good as those teenage rink referees were. They probably weren't even as good as my gauzy memory has made them out to be.

But when the girls laugh and encourage me to try again, I can see so clearly—this is better. For maybe the first time in their lives, my kids are going to see me learn a brand-new, physically challenging skill. That's just not something women of a certain age do very often. My children are going to see me fall and get up and then fall again. Even if it hurts and I risk breaking something. Even if I look silly to both my ten-year-old classmates and their forty-year-old parents. Even if Survival-Me thinks this time would be better spent cleaning the house or helping with homework. The real me, the complete me, the me that lives for adventure, learning new things, taking risks, and laughing easily at both life and herself, is in charge. Life may be tough right now, but I choose this. *This* is what a full life is all about. It's dirty. It's challenging. It's novel. It's whimsical. Sometimes it's painful. But my girls and I are doing it together. And next week, we're headed to the bronze group!

A few minutes later, the girls and I take off our skates and return them to the counter.

"Great job today," the instructor says as she waves goodbye. "See you next week?"

"Oh, we'll be here for the entire six-week session," I say. "This is just too much fun."

CHAPTER 6

CEREAL FOR DINNER AND OTHER SILVER LININGS

ENJOY THE FREEDOM

Drew leaves home for his pre-spaceflight quarantine in June 2019. He isn't gone a week before I completely take over our master bathroom.

"So it seems silly to leave your bathroom stuff out on the counter while you're away, just collecting ten months' worth of dust and gunk. To keep it all clean, I've put it all in a drawer."

"Okay," he says from his home-away-from-home in Star City, Russia. "All I ask is that you put it all back before I get home, so it doesn't seem like you've erased me from the house completely." It's kind of adorable that he worries we'll forget him if I put his toothbrush in a drawer when we have a life-sized cardboard cutout of him in full space suit propped up in the corner of the living room.

"Of course I will," I promise. "When you get back, everything will be exactly as you left it."

And it is. But for the ten months he is away, the master bathroom is my manifest destiny, and luxuriously, all mine.

His sink becomes the temporary home for my hair dryer, flat iron, brushes, and whatever else I happen to toss in there for easy access. I move my makeup bags out of the closet and onto his counter. I take over his towel hook, his section of the shower caddy, and a good portion of his part of the closet. I stick cards with inspirational messages in his mirror. I plug my phone charger into his outlet. I unscrew half the light bulbs on his side of the bathroom to achieve the perfect amount of brightness. I spread out, reveling in my freedom as the only adult using this room. And I am just getting started.

Within a month of returning home from the launch trip in July, I paint two rooms in the house a bright blue color. I hang up new artwork and rearrange the furniture. Drew wouldn't have minded if I'd done it all before he left; I just didn't want to deal with a second opinion. I plan all of our meals around my Monday night dinner delivery and Friday pizza night. Every other night we eat leftovers, something incredibly simple to prepare, or worst-case scenario, another round of mac and cheese or pancakes.

"What do you guys want for dinner tonight?" I ask around 5:50 p.m.

"What can we have?"

"Let's see . . ." I say as I rummage through the fridge and glance in the pantry. "I don't feel like cooking, so it looks like we've got some leftovers and plenty of salad, or you can have cereal."

"Hooray! Cereal again!"

I rarely hear any complaints from the kids about dinner.

While the functionality of the master bathroom goes up and my meal planning skills go down, the most significant changes I implement after Drew leaves revolve around bedtime.

Let me be clear: Drew and I make a great team. We work well together and agree on most things in life. But the most consequential mismatch between us has always been, and probably always will be, bedtime. I love staying up late. I'm a natural night owl, and if something good is on TV, I can stay up forever. I may feel terrible the next day, may even have to literally force myself to fall out of bed to wake up and drink four cups of coffee in order to function, but from my perspective, that's a small price to pay for the pleasure of staying up late. Drew, on the other hand, is an early-to-bed, early-to-rise kind of guy. He's at his sharpest first thing in the morning and likes getting up before everyone else in the family to run, read, or get work done. In his ideal world, we'd both be starting to wind down by 9 p.m. and in bed, dead asleep, by 10 p.m. For me, 9 p.m. is when the night is just getting started. So for two decades, we've bickered over bedtime, usually negotiated to lights-out around 11 p.m. Over the years, when we've joked about our differing bedtime preferences with friends, they've all suggested the same thing: "Why don't you just go to bed at different times?"

What can we say? As corny as it sounds, we like going to bed together. We like moving around each other in the bathroom and turning off the light at the same time. We sleep better together than apart. Going to bed at the same time is something we've done for all twenty-plus years of our marriage. That's just how it is, regardless of the conflict it may cause.

When I turned forty a couple of years ago, I made a list of novel things to try that year. Of all the items on the list, from cooking classes to skydiving, Drew's favorite by far was this one: "Go to bed at 10 p.m. for an entire month."

For years, Drew and other morning people kept telling me how much better my life would be if I went to bed earlier.

"You'll feel more rested!" they'd say. "You'll get so much done the next day! You'll love it!"

So I figured, for my fortieth, I'd put it to the test. For a full thirty days, I was in bed and turned off the light promptly at ten. Every night, as soon as Drew saw me starting to head toward the bedroom, he would stop whatever he was doing and gleefully join me. Every morning, he'd ask me if I slept well, in a voice that implied I'd been cuddled by a bed full of soft golden retriever puppies all night. It was the best month of Drew's life.

I hated every day—and night—of it. I didn't feel better at all. Each and every evening, I'd lie in bed, listening to Drew's deep, comatose breathing, thinking about all the stuff I could be doing and needed to remember to do the next day. Knowing I was losing an extra thirty to sixty minutes every evening, I'd rush around until 9 p.m., losing my valuable mental decompression period. Without that downtime before getting in bed, I'd lie there for an hour, willing myself to fall asleep while my brain performed mental gymnastics. I'll admit that I might not have felt quite so tired in the afternoons, but it wasn't the life-changing experience all those early birds had promised me. So as soon as those thirty days were over, that was it—back to our constant bedtime negotiations.

Not surprisingly, then, every time Drew leaves home for any length of time, my reasonable bedtime is the first thing to go, and this trip was no exception. Almost every night Drew is in space I stay up well past 10 p.m. After the kids go to bed, I settle into the corner of our comfortable couch and binge-watch Netflix until I can hardly keep my eyes open. It is awesome.

"Are you still watching?" Netflix always rudely wants to know after I watch several consecutive episodes.

"I'm insulted you even asked, Netflix. I'm no quitter. Next episode, please."

After I eventually turn off the television, I move into the bath-room where, over the course of several months, I develop a completely ridiculous and utterly frivolous bedtime routine that I could never do if I had to share the space with another person.

Step 1: Turn off all the lights in the house and check to make sure all the doors are locked. Safety first.

Step 2: Do a set of push-ups. Let's work on toning those arms.

Step 3: Slather on a mud mask. It's important to minimize your pores.

Step 4: Read a chapter of a book while you wait for the face mask to dry. Maybe two chapters. Who's counting?

Step 5: Take a long shower. Shave or don't shave—who cares? But do stand under the delightful mist setting from the new showerhead you installed right after Drew left. Ponder life.

Step 6: Wrap yourself in towels and examine your face in the mirror for several minutes.

Step 7: Apply night cream to your face. This one reduces dark spots.

Step 8: Put on your pajamas, the super comfortable, frumpy ones Drew hates.

Step 9: Turn on some music and do a set of lunges in between dancing around the bathroom. Let's have some toned glutes to match those toned arms.

Step 10: Brush your teeth, floss, and rinse. Dental health is super important.

Step 11: Dance around the bathroom for a few more minutes. Why not? You love this song. And the next song. And the one after that.

Step 12: Apply a second type of night cream to your face. You're too young for wrinkles.

Step 13: Climb into bed and grab your book. Prop yourself up with four pillows.

Step 14: Read until the page starts to get blurry or the book starts to drop out of your hands, minimum thirty to forty-five minutes.

Step 15: Turn off the light and settle into the middle of the bed like Cleopatra, surrounded by an excessive number of pillows and your cat. Sleep like the dead.

This is complete bedtime freedom, and I love every single bit of it. Solo once the kids are in bed, I am accountable to no one but myself and God. Sure, there are some mixed results. Understandably, some mornings are a little rough. When the alarm goes off at 6 a.m. and I feel like death because I've chosen to stay up until one, there is no one to blame but myself. But even if I do have to drink an unhealthy amount of coffee to remain upright that day, it is worth it.

Sometimes I feel guilty about enjoying it so much. While I prance around after dark to my favorite music, Drew is sharing a single, vacuum-powered toilet with at least three other people and using a washcloth to bathe for nine long months. As much as I love using his sink, I miss his presence. On any given night, I'd happily give up this luxurious freedom to have Drew back and brushing his teeth next to me. And in the dark recesses of my soul, I know that if he doesn't return home safely to me, this extra space in my bed and my bathroom will feel very different. But I trust he will come home unharmed. For my mental health and the ability to get up every day and function like a healthy adult, I have to. I learned long ago, from friends who had experienced far rougher and longer hardships than mine, that to not only survive but thrive during hard times, you have to look for the silver lining in every storm cloud. They're always there—it's just a matter of finding them.

* * *

While North Carolina summers are nothing compared to those in south Texas, they still get pretty sticky and uncomfortable. When we first arrived in North Carolina in the summer of 2005, it was already too late in the season to do anything to beat the heat, so we made do with kiddie pools and sprinklers. But by the following spring, my friends and I decided that access to an actual swimming pool was a summer necessity. The problem was, none of us had a pool, and there wasn't one in our neighborhood. One of my "bologna is on sale" friends Ashley came up with our solution.

"I found us all the best pool to join. It's inexpensive and convenient, and there's even a diving board."

"Sounds great! Let's all join!"

"There's just one small catch. We're all going to have to become Caribou.[†] They own the pool."

The Caribou Club, or more accurately, the local chapter of the Steadfast and Philanthropic Order of the Caribou, was located on a primo piece of land under the beautiful shady pine trees of the North Carolina Sandhills. I drove by their small sign on an almost daily basis but had never given it much notice. Most of us didn't even know the building was there, let alone a pool.

"There's an application and an initiation ceremony, but if we start now, we can all have our membership cards in hand before the pool season begins."

[†] The name of this service club has been changed. Feel free to substitute the noble animal of your choice.

"Okay," we said. "Tell us what we need to do."

Over the next few weeks, we each trooped over to the lodge to drop off our completed paperwork, which was relatively straightforward. The application simply required I affirm that I (i) was a citizen of the United States, (ii) was at least 21 years of age, (iii) believed in God, and (iv) was not currently a member of the Communist Party. Check, check, check, and check. Ironically, the Caribou organization has not always welcomed women, but among my circle of friends, it was the wives who were applying to be members, not our military husbands. Between deployments, training, and long work hours, it was simpler for us to go through the entire application process than our men. Ashley was the first one through the gauntlet.

"Okay, you guys, you just need to prepare yourself for this initiation ceremony. It's a very serious ceremony, and you might want to laugh, but try to keep a straight face. Remember, it's all for the pool."

A month later, I found myself in the lodge for my initiation ceremony. While the Caribou running the event spoke about the history of the organization, I tried to focus on his words and the loads of commendable, charitable activities this service club participated in each year, rather than the dozens of black-eyed deer heads staring at me from the dark walls of the windowless, wooden-paneled meeting room. I made a mental note to sign up to help with at least one of their admirable community service projects. When prompted by the Grand Master Caribou, I stood and lined up shoulder to shoulder with my ten or so fellow inductees, most likely also joining primarily for pool access. I attempted not to snicker as we repeated the elaborate membership vows, repeating back line after line of antler-pronged oaths. At one point, the man beside me, in an attempt to swallow his amusement as we learned the secret hand gestures, accidentally snorted. I turned and widened my eyes, silently pleading for him to hold it together, lest he spark a tidal wave of uncontrollable giggling from the rest of us so-called "mature" adults.

Later, as we settled into the old seats for the official membership vote, my finger mindlessly flicked the vintage ashtray mounted on the armrest of my chair. Open, close. Open, close. It was easy to imagine the generations of smoke-filled ceremonies that must have taken place there. I would love to say more about what I saw, did, and heard that day, but as the oath I swore warned, if I did so I would risk wandering "through the world forsaken" and being "pointed out as being bereft of decency, unfit to hold communion with true and upright Members." Long story short, I could tell you, but then I'd have to kill you. Besides, I don't remember much. The important thing was that as I stumbled out of that old building two hours later, I was officially a card-carrying "Doe," fully authorized to use the swimming pool for the next twelve months, after which I would be required to pay another year's membership dues and pool fees.

That summer and all the North Carolina summers that followed, my friends and I lounged poolside while our kids splashed in the shallow end. On the way over, we'd swing by the cheapest pizza place in town, get a large cheese pizza to go, and make a night of it. Add a box of goldfish, some grapes, a few juice boxes, and dinner was served. It was cheap, easy, and for a group of women used to our husbands' long hours and frequent trips away from home, it was an essential coping mechanism.

One evening, we began talking about the upcoming deployment cycle, which we knew would soon take several of our husbands away for many months. It would be one of my first deployment experiences, and I was a little nervous.

"Well, here's the thing," one of my friends said. "Instead of thinking about all the things you can't do, you have to focus on what you can do. Instead of focusing on what gets harder, focus on what gets easier."

"Yes!" another seasoned spouse chimed in. "You can make whatever you want for dinner, watch whatever you want on TV, and do whatever you want on the weekends. And the amount of laundry gets cut in half."

"And don't forget the best part!" Lisa jumped in. "Whenever there's something you don't want to do, you can just throw down the deployment card."

Ah yes, the fantastic, albeit metaphysical, deployment card. For the spouses of deployed soldiers, the deployment card is the ultimate get-out-of-jail-free card. Here's how it works: If someone asks you to do something you don't want to do, you just casually throw out the fact that your spouse is deployed, and *poof!*—the discomfort that comes with saying no immediately disappears.

> "Hey, would you like to be room mom this year? It just requires that you ride on a bus with twenty screaming kindergartners for the monthly field trip, plus bring in snacks once a week."
> "Oh, wow, I would love to. But, you know, my husband is deployed right now, so I don't think that's going to work . . ."
> "Oh, of course! No problem!"

> "Hey, would you like to serve on this committee that meets twice a week at night to talk ad nauseam about topics you couldn't care less about?"

"Oh, wow, I would love to. But, you know, my husband is deployed right now, so I don't think that's going to work . . ."

"Oh, of course! No problem!"

You can also use the deployment card to validate any parenting or life decision you make while your spouse is away.

"Drew's away so the kids are going to bed earlier."

"Drew's away so the kids are going to bed later."

"Drew's away so I'm trying out all these crazy recipes."

"Drew's away so I'm serving the same thing for dinner six nights a week."

"Drew's away so I don't care how messy the house gets."

"Drew's away so I'm going to hire a cleaning lady."

"Drew's away so I'm going to take a monthlong trip to see all my family and friends."

"Drew's away so I'm going to tell all my relatives they have to come here to visit me."

"Drew's away so I need to get together with friends at least five times a week."

"Drew's away so I can hole up in my house like a troll and never come out."

I dropped the deployment card in any situation that required justification-removing sorcery to absolve me of my self-imposed mom guilt and false obligations. I'd never felt so much freedom from draining commitments as I did in those deployment months. With the deployment card in my back pocket, ready to be pulled out at any moment, I became the exception to my own rules, the true master of my schedule, and, unburdened of my guilt, more content and confident in my decisions than ever before. I simplified our routine, stressing less about meal planning, doing laundry, and putting toys away. The kids and I read more books, watched more movies, and played more games on the floor. I created more space in my schedule for playdates, phone calls to family, and even the occasional nap. I led my ministry team with a level of efficiency and purpose I'd never reached before, motivated to draw women into the loving community I found such comfort in myself. I prioritized my relationships, and together my friends and I reveled in the positives of this season rather than dwelling on the negatives. They were halcyon days.

As the deployment came to an end, I fretted about what came next. When Drew came home and my deployment card was no longer valid, would I once again get dragged into overcommitting myself to things I didn't even like? Would I once again be guilted into making life harder for myself just because that's what I thought a "good mom" would do? Would I once again lose the freedom to spend time on what fed my soul, connected me to others, and allowed me to invest in myself, my family, and my community?

As an insecure, twentysomething mom, the answer was an unequivocal yes. Once Drew came home, I went right back to my old habits, old obligations, old ways of thinking, and old schedules as quickly as I returned to our regular routines. That wasn't because Drew asked me to or anyone else forced me to; instead, I noticed an internal shift in myself. Dinners got more complicated because I was cooking for two adults instead of one. I felt an internal pressure to be more productive so I had more to report to Drew about what I'd done that day. Without a "valid" excuse to say no, I said yes when asked to serve on teams or take on tasks I had no passion for. I played less and vacuumed more.

But the more time that went by and the more often Drew went away, the more I realized I didn't need a magical deployment card to live in the kind of freedom I felt when I was single parenting. The deployment card was powerful—not because it changed other people's perceptions of me, but because it changed how I viewed myself. It gave me the power and absolution that, for whatever reason, I and many other women often do not feel we have for making our own decisions and bucking the norm. Was I so nervous about having to explain myself or justify my unique choices that I simply went along with the crowd? Was I so scared to tell a friend or stranger "no" that I was willing to overload my schedule with obligations I didn't care deeply about or even like? Was I so afraid of being labeled a "bad mom" by others—or by myself—that I was making choices for our family that I knew were not the best for us? Yes, yes, and yes. But I didn't have to live like this. The truth was, I didn't need Drew to leave the country, or even the driveway, to enjoy that kind of freedom.

The deployment card isn't a tangible thing. It's an empowerment you and I can feel every day, should we choose to embrace it. It's a confidence within ourselves that can be nurtured and grown without the heartache and danger of a combat deployment. It is a freedom to shed the unnecessary burdens of unreasonable expectations, guilt, shame, false obligations, making things more complicated than necessary, and fearing what other people will think. It's the freedom to embrace simplicity, devote our time to what matters to us, invest in relationships instead of possessions, and celebrate the good things in life. It's the freedom to ask God, "What do you want for me today?" and the inner peace to sit in silence while we wait for an answer instead of chasing after social media "likes," the next shiny trophy, or keeping up with the Joneses.

It's paradoxical that many people find the freedom they've been seeking their whole lives only when they hit a season of hardship. Some people develop this confidence after receiving a cancer diagnosis; others when they lose a job or relationship; still others when they lose a loved one. It's as if our suffering allows us to see life clearly for the first time. As we wipe away our tears, we look at the world we have built up around us and question why we've locked ourselves in these cages, thought those things were important, or assumed we would find love, value, or identity in them. Our suffering strips away our false pretenses, false obligations, and false friends. What is left is freedom—the opportunity to explore a world full of possibilities and say with absolute confidence, "This is how I choose to spend my time. This is what is most important. This is what God wants for me."

Jesus quotes from the book of Isaiah when he says,

> He has sent me to proclaim freedom for the prisoners
>   and recovery of sight for the blind,
> to set the oppressed free,
>   to proclaim the year of the Lord's favor.
>
> LUKE 4:18-19

While most of us are not literally imprisoned, blind, or oppressed, we know deep inside that when under pressure and left to our own devices, we often put ourselves in chains, cover our eyes, and limit ourselves. We say yes when we should say no; we pretend we don't see how our ambition, pride, or unrealistic expectations are hurting our family; or we limit ourselves because it's safer to stay in our comfort zone than journey into the unknown. We buy what others buy, do what others do, and say what others say. We do whatever is necessary to avoid hard conversations, think for ourselves, or take ownership of our own choices. We focus on what we don't have and what we can't do, rather than on what we do have and can do. We trade fulfillment for busyness, connection for commitments, confidence for comparison, and peace for harried hustle.

This is not freedom. This is not a reflection of the Lord's favor. Jesus offers, through his presence in our lives, the true freedom to be who he created us to be, to make our own choices, and to own our consequences. He says in essence, *In your trials, in your suffering, let me show you who you are by showing you who I am. I like the real you, not the you who pretends to be someone else, doing what everyone else is doing. I want you—the night owl, late-night snacker, Netflix binge-watcher, midnight bathroom dancer—just as you are. Let me unlock you from your chains. Let me give you some clarity. Let me offer you some kindness. And when this challenging season is over, you can keep these gifts. Take this freedom and put it in your pocket. It's yours.*

* * *

"What have you been talking about with each kid?" I ask Drew during our weekly videoconference a few months into the mission.

"It varies," he says. "They don't have many questions for me anymore. They just want to talk about what's going on at home and school. Sophia spends a good amount of time trying to hold the cat up in front of the camera. Regular kid stuff, I guess. It's like I could be talking to them from anywhere."

"Do you wish they were asking you more questions or were more interested in what you're doing?" I ask.

"Not really," Drew replies. "It's kind of neat that they've just accepted I'm in space and it's not even a big deal anymore. I'm just happy to be their dad, who they simply want to talk to about their day."

By leaning into the freedom offered to me back on Earth, I can offer the best gift I can give Drew while he is in space—the freedom to just be a dad. Drew uses his limited time with the kids each week to stay positive and be an encourager, rather than trying to overcompensate for his absence by back-seat parenting from 250 miles above the Earth. In turn, the kids don't feel abandoned or resentful about him leaving. They adjust because I adjust, taking each new experience in stride and enjoying the freedom to be regular kids with two loving parents, even if one is far from home, floating in microgravity.

Leading up to his launch, Drew and I often spoke about his intangible goals for his mission. They weren't just about science and exploration; we knew this mission had far-reaching implications for our family as well.

"More than anything," Drew told me, "my goal is to return home to a family that is healthy and intact."

"What do you mean?" I asked.

"I mean I want this experience to be just as positive and impactful for you guys back on Earth as it will be for me in space. I want us to feel that our family is stronger and better off because of the mission, not in spite of it."

Drew speaks of this goal often, both with his crew support team and with me. Like Drew, I meet monthly with a crew psychologist who understands the unique rewards and challenges experienced by astronauts and their families. At my appointments with the psychologist, the doctor often says to me, "When I ask Drew how he thinks you're doing with everything, he says you're not just surviving, you're thriving. Is that true?"

"It is," I tell him. "We're making the most of it."

Drew's time in space forces me to hit pause on my fast-paced life and evaluate my choices with renewed clarity. As the only adult in the house, my internal resources feel cut in half and twice as valuable. I want to use my time and energy wisely, investing it where it can have a lasting impact even after Drew returns home. When our family looks back on this time, whether a year or a decade later, I don't want it to be defined by an absent dad and a stressed-out mom. This season is a unique and special gift, full of blessings and opportunities, even if it comes with an equal number of challenges. I don't want to squander this priceless time sweating the small stuff.

Instead of becoming a reactionary, hair-trigger, survival mom who barks orders at her kids and tries to do everything herself, I attempt to let the insignificant things go. I recognize that this season will not, and should not, be the same as when Drew is home. This long-duration mission is an opportunity to make lasting changes for the better.

So I stop fretting about the kids' homework.

I stop trying to keep my floors perfectly clean all the time.

I stop trying to save a few cents by shopping around.

I stop cleaning the house before my friends come over.

I stop going to school, sports, community, or church meetings that aren't required.

I stop worrying if people will wonder why I wasn't there, didn't sign up, or didn't raise my hand.

I stop trying to solve everyone's problems.

I stop doing things other people should be doing.

I stop managing everyone's time.

I stop trying to lead things other people should be leading.

I stop joining, creating, buying, saying, wearing, or being anything just because I think that's what other people are doing.

I should have made these changes long ago. The expectations we put on ourselves build so gradually over time that, like a frog in a slowly heating pan of water, we often don't realize how restrictive the pot we've put ourselves in is until a jolting life event opens our eyes and invites us to reconsider and reset. Leaning into the opportunity this season offers, I reboot my life-management system.

I tell my kids it's their responsibility to get their homework done on time.

I let the house get dusty.

I unsubscribe from a long list of annoying emails and social media accounts.

I teach the kids how to do their own laundry, make their own lunches, empty the dishwasher, and scoop the cat litter.

I ignore the calendar, hanging up holiday decorations early and taking them down late.

I put an old plastic tablecloth on the kitchen table and let kids' craft projects spread out for as long as they're working on them.

I let Amelia cook and make messes in the kitchen.

I let Daniel spend hours in his room creating LEGO masterpieces or reading comic books if that's how he chooses to spend his free Saturday.

I let Sophia and Gabby play outside and explore the neighborhood alone, telling them only to "come back when it's dark."

I delegate significant responsibilities to ministry teammates who've been asking to help me.

After I am done psychologically scrubbing my life, I take all that freshly liberated time and mental energy and reinvest them where they can have a lasting impact on my soul, my family, and my relationships.

I sign up for an exciting committee that needs my skill set.

I complete a giant art project for my own creative outlet.

I plant a garden.

I read twice as many books as I usually do.

I watch every single show of interest on TV.

I set up weekly coffee dates with my local friends.

I call my long-distance friends and family more often.

I spend more time encouraging my ministry team.

I relax more in my hammock.

I slow down.

I have more meaningful conversations.

I feel more grateful.

I feel more fulfilled.

I feel more content.

I become a more considerate wife, patient mom, and generous friend.

I feel more like my authentic self than I have in a long time.

I feel free.

When COVID-19 hits a month before Drew's return to Earth, the schools shut down. Suddenly the kids and I find ourselves stuck at home together while we count down the days until Drew's return. It is just another chapter in the Morgan family's crazy story for that year. But instead of wringing our hands, crying about what we are missing out on, or hoarding toilet paper, we respond by enjoying the freedom this opportunity within an opportunity gives us. We start by watching a movie every night, all five of us snuggled together on the couch under blankets after eating whatever we wanted for dinner, followed by ice cream for dessert.

When Drew walks back in our front door for the first time in almost a year, I know it will mean returning to a reasonable bedtime, trimming back my nighttime routine, cleaning out his sink, and no longer offering cereal as a viable dinner option. But the clarity God has given me about what is most important in life, the new habits I've instilled in our kids, the relationship bridges I've built, and the investments I've made in myself, my friends, my kids, and my marriage will remain. As Drew hoped, we will come out of his mission stronger and better for the experience because instead of simply suffering through it, we have made the most of the readjustment this season offered.

This freedom that God wanted for us, he wants for you, too. When tough times come, don't curl up in a ball, knees tucked up, hands over your head, hoping to hunker down and simply survive until the storm blows over. Stand up, shrug off the weight of the unnecessary burdens you've been carrying, turn into the wind, and go fly a kite. This is freedom.

CHAPTER 7

A 99 PERCENT CHANCE OF AWESOME

EMBRACE THE RISK

It was a regular Tuesday in 2001. Drew and I had been married just over a year, and we were getting ready for the workday. Drew put on his military uniform and made himself cereal for breakfast. I showered and put on one of my many work cardigans and tan khakis as I got ready for my job at a large accounting firm. Drew gathered up his medical textbooks and shoved them into his black backpack before kissing me goodbye on the way out of our apartment in Gaithersburg, Maryland. He was a third-year student at the military medical school located about fifteen miles south in Bethesda.

As Drew opened the front door, he looked back. "Don't forget—tonight's the night I'm bringing the exchange officers over for dinner."

"Of course! I'm ready!"

From the moment Drew had asked me a week earlier if he could invite a few visiting military officers over for dinner, I'd envisioned what the night was going to look like.

"It's one British and two French military medical students," he told me. "They're here in the States to see how our military medical program compares to theirs. I figured it might be fun for them to see how we live, too."

"Absolutely," I agreed. Inside my head, the wheels were already turning. More than anything, I wanted to blow their stylish European socks off. Our apartment was never going to wow them. We lived in a simple, two-bedroom apartment full of hand-me-down furniture from parents and estate sales. But no matter, the food, a classic roast with all the sides, was where I planned to impress them most. My mom was an excellent hostess, and I was determined to follow in her footsteps, even with our tiny apartment kitchen. I'd already purchased everything I needed to create a culinary masterpiece, at least by my twenty-three-year-old standards. As long as I caught the right bus on the way home from work, I should have plenty of time to get the food in the oven, the house dusted, and the living room vacuumed before they arrived. I couldn't wait for the French officers to call up their (I could only assume) adorable, stylish, sous-chef French wives to tell them how this American had fundamentally changed their views of cuisine and hospitality forever.

Just before leaving our apartment, I slipped my feet into a cheap pair of faux-leather penny loafers I'd recently purchased at a discount chain. I grabbed my shoulder bag, locked the door behind me, and headed to the bus stop that would take me to the Metrorail train and then into Washington, DC, for work.

By around 8 a.m., I arrived at my stop on the Red Line, which spit me out a few hundred yards from my office building. I was one of the thousands of people who jostled up the Farragut North Metro station stairs each morning to get to work on time. I was a business consultant at a firm just two blocks from the White House, and it was an exciting area of the city to work in. As the elevator lifted me to our offices on the seventh floor, I mentally prioritized my task list for the day. My project assignment, overseeing an aspect of US rice exports, wasn't exactly thrilling work, but it wasn't terrible either. I stepped off the elevator and strolled to my cubicle, turning on my computer while I tucked my bag under my desk and settled in.

I was barely an hour into the workday when my manager, a tall, stoic woman twenty years my senior, burst into my cubicle.

"A plane has hit a building in New York City," she said in a shaky voice.

"What do you mean? Like a small plane crash?"

"I don't know. I think it was a passenger plane. I'm going to go see if there's more information." She turned and walked away briskly. Even with over a hundred people working on our floor, we didn't have a TV in our break room, so I didn't know where she was headed. I leaned back in my chair, stretching my head out of my cubicle so I could better hear the general murmur of the office. Everything seemed normal.

Must be a terrible accident, I thought. I sat back up and refocused on my spreadsheet.

A short time later a man's yell pierced the silence, followed by a burst of loud talking. A friend and fellow consultant ran down the hallway, pausing slightly when he passed my desk.

"Another plane has hit the World Trade Center in New York! Pull up the news on your computer!"

I swung my chair around, pushing my stack of spreadsheets to the side with one hand while frantically attempting to type the URL for a news site into my browser with the other. The internet was painfully slow, unable to load due to the massive amount of online traffic that had just bombarded the system by people like me looking for information. Finally, I saw a quick flash of the screen as it loaded. I couldn't believe what I was seeing. Pictures of the Twin Towers smoking and burning. Bold headlines crying of terrorism and death. I scanned the page for a minute before the internet crashed again. I stood up and began wandering around the office, looking for someone whose internet was still up. In another cubicle, I joined a small group gathered around a desk with a radio tuned in to a local station. We listened, stunned and sad at the news, but still believing we were removed from a terrible event happening two hundred miles away.

A woman screamed from the far side of the office. "A plane has hit the Pentagon! It's happening here too!"

The Pentagon was less than two and a half miles from where we stood, just over the Potomac River. What had been a distant tragedy was now at our front door. The general concern among my coworkers twisted into full-blown panic, and it was impossible not to be swept up in it. The group of us around the radio scattered back toward our desks. My heart pounding, I sprinted to my cubicle, pulled out my cell phone, and tried to call Drew. I got a recording—the lines were all jammed. My desk phone rang, and I snatched the handset off its cradle.

It was Drew. "Stacey, a plane has hit the Pentagon. They're mobilizing all the medical students in case there are more attacks and they need our help for a mass casualty event." I couldn't believe the words I was hearing him say.

"Oh my gosh, what should I do? Should I leave?" Over the top of my cubicle walls I could see coworkers frantically packing up bags and heading to the door. Blood rushed in my ears.

"Just wait a few minutes and I'll call you back. I'll probably learn something before you do. Hang tight." Then he hung up.

I stood there frozen. We were under attack, and I was afraid for my physical safety in a way I'd never been before. Everyone around me yelled for me to leave with them. I waved them off, calling out that I'd be right behind them. I picked up my bag and put it on my chair, zipping and unzipping the top flap to keep my hands busy. I tried to get on the internet again—no luck. What if Drew couldn't get through to me and I was in danger waiting around for his call? If the terrorists had hit the Pentagon, it was clear what the next target must be—the White House just two blocks away, or maybe the US Capitol, just a little farther down the road. I had to get out of there. I couldn't wait any longer. Just as I threw my bag over my shoulder, my desk phone rang again. I yanked the handset up before it could even ring twice. Thank God, it was Drew again.

"Stace, you need to get out of the city, but don't take the Metro. Just grab your stuff and go. Head toward the medical school, and we'll figure out our next move from there."

I dropped the phone and bolted to the door. I didn't see a single person left on the floor on my way out. I jumped into the elevator, repeatedly pressing the ground floor button with my finger and roaming the small space like a trapped tiger until the doors opened. I burst out of the elevator like a panicked racehorse, running through the lobby and slamming through the glass front doors on my way outside. The scene that greeted me on the sidewalk was unlike anything I'd ever seen before and something I hopefully will never see again. Thousands of people, now including me, had spilled into the streets, all moving in the same northward direction out of the city. We filled the entire street, shoulder to shoulder, all moving in the same direction, like a human wave. As we passed the

Metro station a block away, the crowd around me chattered about the train.

"Do you think the trains are running? That would be the fastest way out of the city."

"Yes, but what if the attackers know that and are waiting for us all to get on and then they bomb it too?"

"You're right! They might. Best to stay above ground and keep walking."

In this new, terrifying, upside-down reality, anything seemed possible. Maybe the train would blow up. Maybe more attackers were waiting with more weapons and more horror. I didn't know it then, but at that moment, several ordinary Americans were literally fighting with terrorists in the sky over Pennsylvania as their hijacked airplane zoomed toward downtown DC. I hustled past the Metro stop, too scared to risk the possibility of something happening underground. I jogged as fast as I could, keeping pace with those around me. It was a beautiful day, not too hot, not too cold, but we were all sweating from fear and exertion. I passed a man wearing a full business suit and carrying a briefcase. Sweat had completely soaked his suit, and the back of his coat was a Rorschach ink blot pattern of dark and light. I settled into a fast walk, not exactly sure where I was going but following the crowd. A man carrying a crying girl, who looked about three years old, passed me on my left. I watched her tiny head bobbing above her father's shoulder as he ran by. Like the rest of us, her tear-stained face registered confusion and uncertainty.

A shop owner had pulled a small television, dialed into the live news coverage, into his doorway. I made my way over, pausing just long enough to see smoke and flames from the Pentagon and the World Trade Center's South Tower collapsing. Some of those huddled around the TV with me were weeping. Some were staring at the screen with blank faces, unable to process what they were seeing. I felt panic rise up in me again. I needed to get out of the city. I moved back into the street and joined the mass exodus once again.

I walked mindlessly, focused solely on heading north toward Bethesda. I didn't actually know how to get there. We had only one car, so I rarely drove downtown. My only plan was to keep walking north and hope that eventually I'd end up somewhere I recognized. Every few minutes, I pulled out my phone and attempted to call Drew, but all the lines were still jammed. As I kept walking, the crowds thinned out with each passing mile. By the time I crossed into Maryland, I was walking alone down the side of a busy road. My feet were killing me. My cheap loafers were coming apart at the seams. I could feel blisters bubbling up on my heels, so when I saw a pharmacy ahead, I crossed the street. When I stepped inside the store, it felt like I'd stepped into yesterday, a time before everything changed. Gentle music played overhead. A bored cashier absent-mindedly picked at his nails. I headed to the first-aid section and grabbed a box of Band-Aids. The cashier slowly scanned the box, seeming not to register how sweaty and rumpled I was. Once back outside, I sat on a bench, pulled off my shoes, and slapped as many bandages on my heels as I could fit. I stuffed the rest in my bag and started walking again. I'd been walking for over ninety minutes, and I still wasn't sure where I was. I checked the phone again. *No service. Keep walking.*

I walked eight miles that day. A mile or so after buying the Band-Aids, I spotted a familiar building in the distance and realized that somehow I'd managed to arrive at the medical school. I took a left and walked along the perimeter security fence. But to my dismay, when I reached the main gate, the guards wouldn't let me in, even with my military ID. Everything was locked down. I wasn't sure what to do next. It was barely noon, but I felt as if I'd been walking for days.

I found a shady spot along the fence and tried Drew again. I was startled when he actually answered.

"Drew! I'm here! But they won't let me in!" I was almost frantic now that I finally had him on the line.

"I know, I've been trying to call you, but it wouldn't go through. Everything is locked down. They aren't taking us anywhere, but they may have us donate blood in case it's needed. Who knows what will happen after that. I have no idea when they'll release us. Just go home. I'll meet you there."

"Okay, I'll meet you at home." I felt better knowing I had another goal to focus on. Just get home.

I knew there was a Metro station across the street from the gate. I walked to it as quickly as I could, but my shoes were a curse. I scanned my Metro card and took the escalator down into the station. As nervous as I had been about getting on an underground train earlier, I knew that only a few hundred yards from the station the train would pop out aboveground, which somehow felt safer. I descended to the ordinarily bustling platform, now abandoned. I waited alone, and when the train pulled in and I got on, I was the only one in the train car. I sat in silence, staring straight ahead. Less than thirty minutes later, I was unlocking our apartment door.

Once inside, I dropped my bag on the floor, took off my shoes, and threw them in the trash. My feet were pink and tender. I filled a bucket with warm water and carried it into the living room, where I turned on the TV. I put my feet in the bucket and glued my eyes to the unbelievable pictures and footage on the television screen. I cried all afternoon, never moving from my spot on the couch or noticing the light outside begin to fade.

Suddenly I heard a key in the lock, and the apartment door swung open. I was shocked when I glanced at the clock and saw that it was now past five. I was even more startled to see Drew walk in, followed by the three foreign medical students he'd invited to dinner days earlier. I sprang up from the couch. I was still in my rumpled cardigan with my pants rolled up past my calves. I wiped my face, tried to straighten my messy hair with my hand, and smiled.

"Hi!" My bag was still on the floor next to the door. The room was dusty and hadn't been vacuumed.

Drew made polite introductions.

"Hi, welcome! Drew, can I talk to you for a minute?" I pulled him into our bedroom.

"I can't believe you still brought these guys home for dinner! With everything that happened today, I figured our plans would have changed."

"How could I not bring them here? They're stuck in a foreign country that has just been attacked, with no family or friends nearby. I couldn't send them back to their hotels alone!"

"Oh, geez, I guess you're right. But there's just one small problem. I didn't do anything to start dinner, and I have nothing else for us to eat."

"Just take the car and go find an open restaurant and get something, anything. I'll stay here with them."

"Okay!" I fixed my pants and threw on some flip-flops. I jumped in the car and started driving a loop past every local restaurant I could think of. *Closed. Closed. Closed.* Finally, I spotted one that was open! *Boston Market will have to do.* I hustled inside, only to find a long line of people with the same idea. By the time I reached the front, most of the serving trays behind the counter were largely empty.

"All we have is meatloaf and corn," the hassled server told me.

"I'll take it," I said.

I grabbed the bag and raced back to the house. The men were in the living room, watching the news coverage. We ate meatloaf and corn off paper plates on the coffee table. We sat and talked for hours, keeping a constant eye on the TV. We didn't know much, but we knew this: The world we lived in was now flipped on its head. As military officers, these men knew that the days of training for conflicts like the Gulf War were over. That playbook had been thrown out. Its rules no longer applied. Our lives would forever be changed.

Within a year, our West Point classmates and friends would be fighting and dying in Afghanistan. Three years later, we would watch as the personal items of a housemate and friend who lived upstairs from our apartment were packed up and shipped back to his family, along with the deepest condolences the US military could offer. Not yet twenty-five, he'd been killed in Afghanistan. His memorial service was the first of many for us.

It would be another year after that before Drew finished his medical education and could finally join the fight. The idea that our friends were risking it all while he was still in training was almost unbearable to him. As soon as he could, Drew put his name forward for an operational assignment with an actively deploying unit. After our friend's death, we knew it was risky. The physical and psychological risk associated with this military career and lifestyle was clear, and the potential cost of service to our nation now seemed far higher than it was when we initially signed on. But together, as a family, we chose to embrace the risk. I think it was then that we began to comprehend what we now know fully—that life is full of risk; some of us are just more aware of it than others.

Many people are surprised to learn that both Drew and I are not natural risk-takers. We admit that we look like people who throw caution to the wind. Adventure travel, skydiving, scuba diving, military deployments, rocket launches—we get it. On paper, we look like risk lovers. But we're really not. What we are, in truth, is experienced risk evaluators. Over the years, we have taken a hard look around at the world and embraced the fact that risk is unavoidable. It's an inherent part of life, whether we like it or not. But instead of running from it, talking each other out of it, protecting our children from it, or pretending it doesn't exist, we've learned to harness that risk to live lives of adventure that are full of meaning and purpose. Before Drew's space launch, I heard more than one reporter ask him if, given his high-adventure résumé, he considered himself a thrill seeker.

"No, I consider myself a calculated risk-taker," Drew replied, which is 100 percent true.

In fact, we are a family of calculated risk-takers. We've decided that there aren't just a few things in life worth taking a risk on, there are many.

* * *

Eight months before Drew's launch into outer space, I decided to go skydiving. Full disclosure: This wasn't my first time. When I first met Drew, he was an active skydiver, so I've had years to slowly acclimate to the idea of jumping out of a perfectly good airplane. About a year after we got married, I actually did it. Strapped to a tandem instructor, I fell out of an airplane at thirteen thousand feet. Drew jumped solo right behind us. Other than the extreme wind and my excessive screaming, I don't remember much about that day, but I do recall how amazing I felt when we landed back on the ground. For a split second, I understood why some people want to do this every day, over and over again. It was absolutely exhilarating.

So when I was drafting my list of exciting, fun, and unusual things to do when I turned forty, I remembered that feeling and decided I wanted to experience it again. The thing was, it had been almost twenty years since that first jump. Back then, Drew and I had no kids, no house, no financial assets to speak of, not even a goldfish. If something happened to me, Drew would undoubtedly have been devastated, but there wouldn't have been the layers of life logistics to unravel like there were now. Now I was a mom of four children, a cat owner, a ministry leader, a minivan driver, and a cosigner on a mortgage. Even Drew was a little uneasy with the idea at first.

"Are you sure this is wise? I mean, the kids need me, but they *really* need you."

"Do I have to remind you how ridiculous it is for you to be saying *this* is too risky? You, the guy who's about to launch into space?"

"Well, when you put it like that . . ."

I brought him around to the idea pretty quickly. My friends were harder to convince. As I do with all my crazy ideas, I invited my friends to join me. Instead of immediately signing up with me, most felt it more appropriate to make sure I understood exactly how skydiving works.

"You do know you have to jump out of an airplane, right?"

"If the parachute doesn't open you will die when you hit the ground, if you don't have a heart attack on the way down first."

"My cousin says he knows a guy whose coworker's sister had a neighbor who almost died skydiving!"

I was unmoved. Years of flipping through Drew's *Parachutist* magazine made me well aware of the statistics. But just to be sure, I conducted a quick risk assessment and looked up the current statistical likelihood of dying while skydiving. I was pleasantly surprised to learn there's a less than 0.000005 percent chance of becoming a skydiving fatality.[8] You'd have to do a lot of dangerous skydiving stunts and a lot of rounding up to get that number even close to one percent. I told my friends this.

When they saw I was undeterred by their skydiving horror stories, some switched to a new tactic—mom guilt.

"Are you sure you should do this? What would *your kids* do without you if something happened??"

"I know you *say* it's safe, but nothing is 100 percent safe. Are you really willing to take that chance?"

"Think about how devastating it would be to *your children* if something happened to you."

"I think it's great *you* want to do it, but I could *never* do that."

They almost got me when they brought the kids into it. Their warnings spoke to the reasonable, calm voice in my head that, whenever I get an itch to do something wacky or unexpected, encourages me to sit down and have a cup of tea instead.

Reasonable-Me focused on that less than one percent chance of something horrible happening and had it all worked out: *Listen, girl, your friends are right. Skydiving is a bad idea. Anything that risks your life, even if just a tiny percent chance, is too much. Think of your children! Sometimes Drew needs help to remember where everything goes when he empties the dishwasher. He can't raise these children alone! How would they live without you if something happened? THINK OF THE CHILDREN! You can't take these kinds of chances. A good mom, a responsible mom, wouldn't even think about doing this. So how about this—let's forget this ever happened. Let's just pretend you never thought of this crazy idea and get back to focusing on the most important things in life, like what's for dinner. What do you think? Tacos?*

I almost gave in. It would have been easier and cheaper to just let it go. I almost let my fear of what might happen, or what my friends might think of me, win me over. I was *this close* to scrapping the whole irresponsible idea when a text from my friend Allison grabbed me by the shirt and pulled me back over the line.

"I'm IN," her message read.

At that moment, the other voice in my head, Bold-Me, the one who thinks up these zany ideas, sat up straight in the recliner she lounges on in the back of my mind. She likes to whisper her grand ideas in my ear but then immediately backs down when Reasonable-Me pipes up and reminds her of our family obligations and social responsibilities. Having now processed the fact that Allison is all in, Bold-Me jumped up out of her chair and roared like a gladiator.

"That's my girl!" Bold-Me bellowed. "Allison knows what's up! I bet you have a higher chance of dying on the way to IKEA than you do skydiving. Let's do this!"

Just to be sure, I looked up that statistic too. And you know what? Bold-Me was right. I have a much greater likelihood of dying in a car wreck on my way to IKEA than I do skydiving. But you didn't see my friends trying to talk me out of driving up to Houston to buy a new set of Fjälkinge shelves. From that moment on, I drew a line in the sand. I reaffirmed that I didn't want to live my life focused on the one percent chance of failure, whatever that failure might be. Instead, I wanted to live my life in bold anticipation of the 99 percent chance of mind-blowing, bucket list–blasting success. Because I believe in my bones that this is the kind of life God wants for me, and even if I do fail, at least I'll go down trying.

"Yeeeessssssss." I texted Allison back with about eighteen emoji hearts and twenty-three fist bumps. "Let's do this."

Why do we act like such scaredy-cats sometimes? Why do we accept risk in the dull, inconsequential parts of our lives, like driving on the highway at night, climbing a ladder to hang Christmas lights, or eating expired yogurt, but then reject it when it's attached to something new and exciting? Why do we limit ourselves and talk ourselves out of taking risks? I am keenly aware that my life, primarily through my marriage to Drew, carries a higher level of physical risk than most people's. His deployment experiences alone put us into a category of risk management that only a small percentage of military people—and insurance adjusters—genuinely understand. Add rockets and space travel to the equation, and life starts to feel a little fragile. But physical risk isn't, by far, the only or scariest type of risk out there. Ask anyone who's contemplated making a major career change, breaking off a relationship, moving across the country, getting married, starting a business, adopting a baby, writing a book, having a hard conversation, or saying "I love you." They'll tell you that there are endless events in life that feel very risky while still keeping our feet planted firmly on the ground.

The more mature and responsible we get, the less risk most people are willing to tolerate. As we grow our families, work our way up the ladder, widen our circles, and expand our repertoire, most of us see reducing our exposure to risk as a goal within our greater life plan of attaining increased ease and comfort. The more of this harsh life we experience and the more sad stories we hear about those who gambled it all and lost, the more we want to lock ourselves behind our protective walls, stay in our lane, keep our mouths shut, and risk nothing.

Sometimes I've let my fear of risk take up more space in my heart and mind than it should. It's a tempting trap. When you have higher levels of risk in one area of life, the natural tendency is to overcompensate with extra safety and security in another. In other words, if Dad has a high-risk job, Mom should stay at home wrapped in layers of Bubble Wrap. We are afraid to risk it all, so most of us risk zero. On the surface, playing it safe seems to cost us nothing. We simply choose to stay seated, keep our hands in our laps, and not participate. Life goes on, as predictable as ever. What we don't realize is that every time God places a soul-vibrating opportunity in front of us and we say no because the risk feels too great, we have already lost.

The truth is, as 9/11 so tragically brought to light, we live in a world full of unknown dangers and potential tragedy. There is no such thing as a risk-free life. Some of us are just more aware of that fact than others. Spending our physical and mental energy attempting to dodge every bullet is exhausting, mainly because we never see most of those bullets coming. Instead of fearing risk, what if we made it something we look for, a harbinger of adventure or an indicator of where God is prompting us to go? What if we uncoupled risk from fear and attached it to faith? What if we stopped playing it safe and instead fully embraced the apostle Paul's confidence when he declares to his younger ministry partner Timothy, "For the Spirit God gave us does not make us timid, but gives us power, love and self-discipline" (2 Timothy 1:7).

Paul isn't sanctioning reckless, dangerous behavior that could harm others. He's encouraging a posture of courage, wanting us to be unafraid to take risks in order to live full lives and step onto the path God has for us. Paul is a calculated risk-taker, using God's power, love, and self-discipline in his life to strengthen his backbone. He's calling us to a life of grit and spunk. God wants a people unafraid to jump into the deep end of life, fueled by his bold love and tenacious faith. God uses people willing to embrace risk and takes them on daring adventures. I don't want to be left out.

* * *

Early on our skydiving morning, I picked Allison up and we drove to the drop zone. We strolled into the skydiving hangar, where we checked in and a woman handed us a stack of legal documents to sign. As we sat down at a table and began scribbling away our lives, my cell phone vibrated in my pocket. Two of our friends were asking to FaceTime. We clicked Accept, and their pretty faces smiled back at us.

"Hey! Are you at the drop zone yet? We just wanted to see if you were really going through with it!" They were sitting on a front porch, drinking coffee.

"Yeah, we are! And we both bought the video package, so you're going to have to watch the videos of our jumps a dozen times." We fanned our waivers in front of the camera and swiveled the phone to show the other brave people in the room. "It's going to be awesome. You're going to regret you didn't join us." Looking at their faces, a mixture of disbelief and awe that we were actually doing it, I think a tiny part of them already did.

We handed in our forms and headed to the side of the hangar, where we were introduced to our young but highly qualified tandem instructors. We were not quite old enough to be their mothers, but we could definitely have been their babysitters. They handed us our flight suits, and Allison and I laughed as we helped zip each other up. Nylon skydiving suits are, for sure, the least flattering article of clothing on the planet for all body types. As we stepped into our harnesses and pulled up the arm straps, we heard a commotion in the parking lot. Our husbands had arrived with our six kids in tow. The younger ones skipped across the gravel, skidding to an abrupt stop when they saw us standing with our instructors in all our gear.

"Hey, guys, you're just in time!"

As a gaggle, eight pairs of eyeballs watched us practicing our hand signals and pulling the rip cord. The kids wandered over to touch the metal clips on our harnesses, examine the altimeters on our wrists, and try on our goggles. The adrenaline in the hangar kept everyone upbeat, but as we got closer to jump time, I could see some apprehension on the kids' faces: *Are they actually going through with this?* Our husbands, both reserved personalities, hung off to the side in strong but silent support. Next to me, I could feel Allison's nervous energy radiating off her. My own apprehension, plus the fact that this was my big idea, made me overcompensate by hamming it up for the camera and cracking jokes as we posed for pictures, talking louder and laughing harder than I should.

We snickered when the videographer pulled Drew over for a mock interview. "What do you think of your wife jumping out of an airplane today? Think that's something you'd like to try someday?"

"Probably not," Drew said with a wink. "I'm pretty risk-averse."

Our instructors told us it was time to load up, so we kissed the men and kids, waving goodbye as we paraded toward the waiting airplane. With one last salute as we left the hangar, our families moved to the grassy viewing area next to the large open field out back where we planned to land in all our parachute glory in about thirty short minutes.

Allison and I, along with our tandem instructors and the rest of our jump mates, lined up and piled into the aircraft. I was the last student in. There was a skinny bench along each wall of the small airplane. As the last to board, I was left with the last eight inches of the bench closest to the door, facing the back of the plane. I sat down and scooched myself back as far as I could, realizing with a gulp that this meant I'd be the first one out. I turned and gave Allison a quick smile, the rotor-engine noise too loud to talk over. She had a blank look on her face, like she wondered how the heck she'd ended up there.

With a jolt, the plane began rumbling down the grass runway, and once it gained enough speed, pulled up sharply into a steep incline.

I felt my nylon-covered bottom slide a few inches down the bench toward the door. I stuck out my foot to brace myself so I wouldn't slide off the edge and right out the still-open door. My active imagination could easily see it happening. I turned to peer out the tiny window next to my right shoulder and was amazed at how high we already were. Looking down at the altimeter strapped to my wrist, I could see we were only a third of the way to thirteen thousand feet, and my stomach was already churning. The videographers knelt on the floor in front of us, joking among themselves while one of them casually slid the door closed. With hundreds, if not thousands, of jumps under their belts, this was just one more entry for their logbook, no big deal. As I stared out the window, watching the ground get farther and farther away, I thought this might have been one time too many for me.

As we approached jumping altitude, the videographers squeezed down the aisle between our knees, prompting us to give excited high fives and thumbs-up. Allison and I waved to the camera, but I could tell from the tightness in her smile that she felt the same way I did. I'd forgotten how terrifying this moment is—the minute you second-guess every decision that brought you here but realize it's too late to back out.

The jumpmaster threw open the door and waited for the small light on the wall to switch from red to green. I watched it too, knowing that once it flipped, I would be the first victim. The wind from the open door whipped through the cabin, blowing my hair across my face. Behind me, I could feel my instructor snapping the carabiners on the back of my harness to the front of his, and he reached around me to cinch the straps down tight. I pressed back against him, any awkwardness from a forty-year-old woman snuggling up to her twenty-year-old instructor wholly negated by my primal desire to tighten one more inch of slack out of the straps and avoid death.

The light flashed green, and my instructor grabbed my arms and crossed them over my chest while we spider walked the short distance to the door. He held the thin bar bolted across the top of the exit, arching his back so I arched with him. My toes hung off the edge of the door, and half of my body was already outside the airplane. The only thing keeping us from falling out was my instructor's fingers on the bar. To my left, I could see my videographer, hanging outside the door, his right foot positioned on a thin ledge outside the airplane, ready to follow us into the blue once my instructor let go. I snapped my head to the right, and from over my instructor's arm I could see Allison's face, staring at me with a look of horror at the realization that once I went, she was next. I shot her a quick panicked look, followed by what I hoped was a reassuring smile, before my instructor reached down, pulled my forehead back toward his face, and then leaped forward, propelling us out and away from the plane.

It was all wind and screaming and terror and exhilaration. I instantly forgot everything my instructor had told me to do. I pulled my legs forward instead of back into an arch. I looked down instead of keeping my head up. I felt the instructor and me wobble as we fell, spinning and unstable in the air, thanks to my lack of body position awareness. I could feel him attempting to stabilize us as he threw out the small drogue parachute designed to slow us down as we plummeted back toward the Earth. His action jolted me back to reality, and I remembered what I was supposed to do. I pulled my arms and legs back into an arch and lifted my chin, slightly surprised to see the videographer already hovering in free fall directly in front of me, the camera strapped to his helmet recording every terrifyingly fantastic second. He waved and I waved back, then made a heart shape with my fingers and smiled for the camera.

Well, now you're just showing off, Responsible-Me said. She had locked herself in the closet with her hands over her eyes and ears until this was all over while Bold-Me whooped it up, throwing popcorn in the air and begging me to flash a few peace signs to the camera during the last few remaining seconds of free fall.

Then the instructor tapped my arm and pointed at my altimeter, meaning it was time for me to reach back and pull the rip cord for the pilot chute that would, in turn, pull out the main parachute. In the blink of an eye, the large blue parachute canopy was out and instantly inflated, snapping our legs out in front of us as we abruptly slowed from our 120 mph terminal velocity speed to a pleasant 20 mph. The roar of the wind ceased, and my instructor and I chatted as we enjoyed the scenery, pulling the parachute toggles together to steer us in big lazy circles toward the drop zone.

Back on the ground, Drew and the kids watched as the plane roared into the air, and with hands raised to shield their eyes from the bright sun, they saw the tiny speck that was my instructor and me somersault out into the cloudless sky. They watched in rapt attention as we dropped closer and closer and gasped in surprise and relief when my bright blue parachute fluttered out and filled with air. And when my wonderfully talented instructor steered us to our final destination by dramatically zooming us right over their heads and outstretched arms, the kids erupted in cheers and jubilation. We landed dead center, right in front of them, like death-defying circus performers. Less than a minute later, Allison landed just a few feet away, a perfect finale. We laughed and shouted to each other in overwhelming joy. Once our instructors unhooked us, we rushed together, bear hugging and high-fiving each other with broad grins. Then we turned and embraced our instructors in the same overly enthusiastic way. The professionals gathered up our parachutes and headed back toward the hangar while Allison and I strutted into the viewing area, the conquering heroes. The kids hugged us, excited by us and for us. They peppered us with questions, gripping our hands and hanging on to every detail.

Back in the hangar, it took only a few minutes for the video editors to finish our highlight reels. We watched them both twice, the kids' eyes wide with disbelief when they saw their mom on the screen being so brave, taking a chance, having her own adventure, and seemingly risking it all. When the video ended, something unexpectedly wonderful happened; each of my kids turned to me and asked how old they had to be before they could make their first jump. I'd forgotten that one of the most potent side effects of living unafraid and taking risks is that it inspires those around you. My willingness to be brave, try something new, and literally take a leap of faith made my kids want to do the same. Even more than wanting to embrace risk in my own life, I want to raise children who are willing to take risks in their own lives. Over the years, I've told them with my words that I don't want them to live in fear, that all good things in life require sacrifice, and that it's better to try and fail than never to have tried at all. But how often have I modeled those words? Without action, my words are empty platitudes. On this day, I proved, in one small way, that I mean what I say.

I could see their wheels turning. *My mom jumped out of an airplane!*, their inner dialogue said in astonishment. This day shifts their axis a little, back toward the risk-calculating but not risk-fearing orientation I want them to keep. I'd inspired them that day, but it couldn't stop here. As parents setting the example for our children, and as people embracing all life offers us so we can join with God in the miraculous and amazing things he is doing, we must continue to live lives full of risk. We must pledge to be unafraid of the world.

We must challenge ourselves, seek out adventure, and have faith. We must live in hopeful anticipation of the 99 percent chance of something awesome happening.

"You have to be eighteen to skydive," we told the kids. They moaned in disappointment. "But we'll make this deal with you: On your eighteenth birthday, if you still want to do it, we'll bring you here for your first jump. And we'll jump with you."

CHAPTER 8

HITTING THE WALL

HAVE FAITH

Just three months before Drew's launch, we receive the official word: His mission will be extended past the usual six months. Instead of the standard two space expeditions, he'll be on the ISS for three—Expeditions 60, 61, and 62—for a total of 272 days. NASA started lengthening space missions beyond six months only recently. In fact, of the more than 360 American astronauts who have flown in space, fewer than ten have stayed in orbit for over two hundred days in one single spaceflight. While 272 days pales in comparison to the 365-plus days our military friends often spent deployed, the kids and I have never been separated from Drew this long. In fact, no American with such a large family has been in space so long before. In that sense, we are blazing a new, somewhat bumpy trail.

Halfway into Drew's nine-month space mission, he and I hit the wall. If you're a runner or any kind of endurance athlete, then you know what "hitting the wall" means. It's the point at which your body, in complete cahoots with your brain, tells you, *We need to stop. This is too hard. Let's just sit down and never get back up again.* Physically, "hitting the wall" often feels like heavy legs, labored breathing, and extreme exhaustion. Mentally, it's an intense desire to just lie down on the pavement and die. Your pace slows to a crawl, you can't think straight, and you feel terrible. Everything inside of you is begging you to quit this hard thing you are doing. There are many reasons runners might hit the wall, but while Drew is away, I learn you can also hit the wall floating in space or sitting on your couch.

The first few months of Drew's mission are a flurry of activity for both of us. The schedule is always packed on the space station, but that season is exceptionally busy. The crew completes an unusually high number of spacewalks and has literally tons of cargo to unload, sort, and stow from several visiting resupply spacecraft. The crew also must manage and maintain a large number of demanding science experiments. Free time is in short supply, and there is always something else that needs to get done before the crew can rest.

"Today was the longest day ever," Drew tells me regularly.

"Why?" I ask. "Don't they limit the number of hours you work each day?"

"Yes, but that doesn't account for exercise, breaks to eat a quick lunch or go to the bathroom, and a handful of other random tasks we have to do. When it's all said and done, we end up with very full twelve-hour days."

"Did you get a chance to look out the window at the Earth or take pictures today?"

"Not today or yesterday. There was just too much work to do. And after the official day ends, I still need to do everything most people would do during their regular workday, like answer emails and make phone calls."

"Did you at least have dinner with everyone tonight?"

"Yeah, we ate together like we do most nights. Then we cleaned up and I called you, but I still have to brush my teeth and get ready for bed. Hopefully I'll have a little time to decompress before turning off the light. These days move quickly because they're so jam-packed, but it's like the day just goes on and on and on . . ."

"And then you start it all over again the next day."

"Exactly."

With few windows, no natural cues like temperature changes or wind, sixteen sunrises and sunsets every twenty-four hours,[9] and long, busy workdays, Drew's perception of time takes on a strange new pace. Very little about his environment changes on a daily or weekly basis, making the long days creep by slowly and blend together. Drew feels the change in his perception of time most acutely when talking to us about our lives back on Earth. We jokingly call it the "*Interstellar* effect" after the Matthew McConaughey movie in which the main character returns from his space mission after a year, only to find that more than seventy years have passed on Earth. Time seems to be standing still for Drew while our lives on Earth are jumping ahead of his. He confesses that sometimes it feels as if he is missing out on important milestones in our kids' lives. I tell him I get it—it is hard enough for me to keep up with all four of our kids' growth spurts, relationship changes, and schoolwork, and I live with them!

Back at home, the early fall is crammed full of sugar-laced birthday parties; back-to-school pencil sharpening; packing and unpacking for work travel; boisterous junior high church events; chlorine-scented swim meets; Texas-spirit-sized football games; sweaty marching band competitions; and more days spent at mission control watching

Drew's spacewalks than I ever thought possible. From the moment Drew arrived on the station and the kids and I returned home, we've all been in a flat-out sprint. I started keeping two calendars—one paper, one digital—just to keep my life straight. If an event wasn't on both calendars, it wasn't happening.

"So I completely dropped the ball today," I tell Drew about a month into the mission. "I was headed to a work event tonight when I got a text asking me if I was on my way to the high school to pick up band uniforms. Whoops."

"Oh man!" Drew says. "What did you do?"

"I apologized for forgetting about it, but I was pretty embarrassed. Now I have to show up tomorrow to pick up these uniforms in the middle of the school day when all the high schoolers are there; it'll be like a band mom walk of shame. I had forgotten to put it on my second calendar, so I missed it completely. And by the way, I measured Daniel and he's officially taller than you now."

"No way, that can't be," Drew says. "I was taller than him just a couple of months ago!"

"Such is the power of puberty," I reply. "I have to get him some new jeans. The ones he has look like capri pants, and I can't let him leave the house like that."

"By the time I get home he's going to be towering over me!"

"Yep, I think you need to start mentally preparing yourself for not being the tallest in the family when you get home."

Life moves so fast that Drew has to work doubly hard not to get left behind. To keep up with the seemingly infinite string of family birthdays, Drew calls the kids on their special day to say happy birthday and chat before they leave for school. He wrote each a birthday card in advance and left it behind for me to give them on the big day. To reassure him that I am tracking his life as closely as he is tracking ours, I email him pep talks and messages telling him how proud I am of him on the days I know he has hard tasks or interviews scheduled. Our lives seem like bullet trains, and as we hang on by our fingernails, we remind each other that this is a marathon, not a sprint, even if we both secretly worry about how long we can keep up this breakneck pace.

After commiserating during one of our video chats, I ask Drew, "Remember when I told you the story about running the marathon and being cheered on by my friends?"

"Yeah, of course."

"Just when the wheels were starting to come off, they appeared and yelled, 'You're doing it!' and that made all the difference. I think this mission is like that. When things start to get crazy, we can't forget: We're doing it!"

"We're doing it," he echoes.

We both jam what seems like a year's worth of activity into the mission's first four months. Then Thanksgiving rolls in. The work pace on the space station slows down for a day or two, so Drew can finally catch his breath. My relatives fly into town, the kids go on holiday break, and my work pauses for the week. Both of us eat turkey with jellied cranberry sauce, send pictures of our Thanksgiving meals to each other, and admit we are a bit mentally tired. Then we look at the calendar and realize that after four incredibly busy months, we still have over half of the mission to go. Cue the wall.

"Hey," Drew mumbles when I answer the phone at the end of the holiday weekend.

"Hey. What's up? You sound tired."

"I'm just looking at the pictures you sent and thinking about how much I miss you guys."

"Didn't you have a good Thanksgiving with your crewmates?"

"Yeah, it was great, but I was looking at these pictures and thinking about how I wasn't there for your birthday, or Soph's birthday, or Daniel's birthday, or the start of school, or Thanksgiving, and how I won't be there for Gabby's birthday or Christmas. That makes me sad."

"I'm sorry you feel that way. Is there anything I can do to make you feel better? Anything I can send you?"

"No, I don't think so. When I look at the calendar, it's a little depressing. There's still so much more time to go. It feels like forever."

I hate that he feels left out, like time is leaving him behind. In all the prep for the holidays, I hadn't really considered that aspect of his mental health. My life with four kids is so fast paced that I've been spending all my mental energy trying to keep all the balls in the air, not figuring out ways to keep Drew from feeling as if the kids are growing up without him. I resolve to be more intentional about keeping him updated on Christmas preparations and all the holiday bustle.

My holiday season feels as hectic as any other year, perhaps even more so. I want to make it even more magical and meaningful for my kids because their dad is gone. I decorate the house in early December, hauling the Christmas tree downstairs by myself and climbing ladders to string lights and hang garlands. We plan to fly to Pennsylvania to celebrate with family, which means added logistics for ordering and wrapping presents early, closing up the house, and finding a cat sitter, on top of the usual cookie making, Hallmark Christmas movie watching, and the kids' midterm exams just before the holiday break. It is a whirlwind of tinsel-draped, tiresome work, trying to keep Christmas exciting and enjoyable for the kids while not making Drew feel even more down than he already does. As pleasurable as the holidays are, part of me will be relieved when they end and we can go back to our boring routine with nothing special for Drew to regret missing.

"Did you watch the Christmas video we sent you?" I ask him on December 26. I had spent an hour compiling all our pictures from Christmas Day into a video slideshow set to Drew's favorite holiday songs.

"Yes, it was great. But I could only watch it once—it was just too tough to see what I was missing. Maybe later I'll be able to watch it again, but not now."

Though I try so hard to make Drew feel connected to what we are doing, in some ways it has the opposite effect because it gives him an even closer look at what he's missing. As unique and meaningful as his Christmas is on the station, it isn't home and he isn't with his family. In the holiday gloom period, his days feel extra long, his tasks feel extra hard, and simply put, he misses us. As incredible as it is to be floating in space, he just wants to come home, listen to Christmas music, and open presents with us by the tree. He has hit the wall.

January eventually arrives, and I take all the decorations down. I haul the Christmas tree back upstairs into storage. I drink my last eggnog latte. I eat the last Christmas cookie. Then I sit in my now cheerless living room feeling tired and glum. Now that the hustle is over, time seems to stand still. It feels as if Drew left a lifetime ago, and yet months and months remain before he comes home. After staying in a house full of holiday visitors and a dozen cousins, I feel lonely and alone. With all the Christmas warmth, sparkle, and nostalgia put away until next year, my house feels cold, bland, and boring. I look out the window and see gray sky and brown, dormant grass. Everything is blah. There is nothing on the next several pages of my desk calendar to look forward to. Nothing exciting to plan for.

Not even anything good for dinner. *This stinks*, I think. *And there's no end in sight.*

I have hit the wall.

* * *

In 2012 I had one of my crazy ideas—I decided to run a marathon. At the time, I was a slow and steady recreational runner at best. A few months before, Drew and I had entered a local 5K fun run because we wanted the free T-shirt and we read in a marriage book that we should find more "active" hobbies to do together. We stuck around for the awards ceremony for the sole purpose of eating more free snacks. I almost choked on my complimentary, post-race banana when I heard my name announced as a race winner. Remarkably, I was the top female finisher between the ages of 30 and 35! There were only three of us in that category, but that didn't matter to me. I was delighted when they handed me an impressive trophy with a spread-winged, fierce-looking silver eagle on top, which I paraded home as if it were the Stanley Cup. I plopped it on the kitchen table, proudly announcing to the children that I had beaten every other person in my bracket, which was true.

A couple of months later, I met a fellow military wife named Julie. She appeared to be the same age and fitness level as me, but she had far more long-distance running experience. She casually mentioned she was looking for a marathon training partner.

"You are?" I said. "I could be your training partner if you tell me what to do. The longest I've ever run is a half-marathon, and that was years ago."

"No problem," she said. "If you can run a half, you can run a full. We can start next week." Her naive confidence in my running abilities should have been my first indication that this was going to be harder than it looked.

Talk to anyone who's ever run a marathon, and they'll tell you that it's not the race that kills you, it's the training. It takes forever to work up to 26.2 miles if you've run nothing longer than a 5K fun run lately. As the race approaches, you need to be able to run at least twenty miles, which takes hours—a long time to run without someone to talk to. I figured I might never find another training partner like Julie, plus Drew's job as a sports medicine fellow left most of his weekends free, so he could watch the kids. Finally, as my majestic trophy reminded me every time I walked by it, I was now a race winner, not just a race participant. The stars were never going to align better, so it was now or never.

Julie emailed me a training plan that required both of us to run several times during the week, then complete a long run together on Saturday mornings. If we stuck to the plan, we'd be ready for the Marine Corps Marathon in Washington, DC, in late October. Every Saturday morning we met at the start of the Mount Vernon Trail, a beautiful paved path that meanders along the Potomac River. Julie kept our running pace and told me when it was time to turn around and head back toward our cars. Every weekend for months we ran, talking about life and comparing the best-tasting energy bars. The training was grueling, and every time I pulled into the empty parking lot at 5:30 a.m. I was reminded that there was no way I could have maintained this level of discipline by myself. Every Saturday morning, I was so tempted to pull up the covers and stay in bed, but the thought of Julie waiting for me in that dark, predawn parking lot provided just enough guilt and motivation to get me moving. As our mileage increased and the race day drew nearer, my excitement grew. But a few weeks before the race, Julie dropped a bomb.

"So on race day I'm really going to pick up my pace. I'll need a sub-3:30 in order to qualify for Boston."

"Wait, what?" I said. "You are trying to qualify for the Boston Marathon?" This may have been my first marathon, but I knew that qualifying for Boston was no small feat. If she did it, she'd be running a lot harder and a lot faster than I was capable of.

"Yeah, I've been pacing myself on my shorter runs, and I think I can do it."

"That's amazing! I know you'll make it," I said to her face. But inside, my fantasy of us jogging along and enjoying a carefree chat for the entire 26.2 miles before holding up our clasped hands in triumph while crossing the finish line together went up in a giant puff of smoke. In Julie's defense, she'd probably mentioned Boston before and I just hadn't been paying attention. I was so focused on simply surviving our long runs and letting her mentally pull me along, I blocked out anything that didn't fit into my "finish the marathon with a friend" narrative.

Maybe she'll change her mind if I enrapture her with extra delightful conversation and plenty of witty jokes between now and then, I told myself.

She didn't.

I fretted endlessly about running the race solo. I had no false aspirations about my marathon performance. Five hours of running by myself? Impossible. On an almost daily basis, I googled "marathon survival tricks" for anything that might help me. One suggestion caught my eye: Spectators love to cheer for runners, but they don't know who you are! Write your name in big letters on the front of your shirt so those who see you run by can yell your name out in encouragement. I loved this idea. I thought it seemed entirely reasonable that strangers might want to cheer me on by name. Plus, I knew I'd need as much confidence boosting as I could get, and it didn't matter to me where I got it from. I ordered a custom race T-shirt with

"STACEY!" and a picture of a turtle printed on the front. On the back of my shirt were the words "Marathon goal time: Finish with dignity." That pretty much summed it up.

Julie sensed my trepidation about running alone and mercifully offered to introduce me to two friends of hers who were coming into town for the race. She said they planned to run at a pace similar to mine, and though I didn't know them, the idea of running by myself was so heinous I said I'd love to meet them.

The morning of the race was a beautiful, crisp October day. Julie and I found each other near the race entrance and amazingly enough, ran into her two friends soon thereafter. Julie made some quick introductions, and we chatted nervously, hugging our arms to stay warm in the early morning air before heading to the starting corrals. The elite runners were much farther up the road, under the starting line banner, which seemed miles ahead of us. We could barely hear the announcer's voice from the huge speakers when he told us the race was about to begin. Even after we heard the crack of the starting pistol, it was a full fifteen seconds or more before the initial movement wave reached our section and we surged forward. Packed shoulder to shoulder, the starting pace was slow, but Julie took off quickly, and we watched as her head weaved through the crowd away from us.

"See you at the finish!" we yelled. "You can do it!"

For the first few miles, running with these two new best friends wasn't so bad. The mass of runners that surrounded us forced me to slow my pace, which felt pretty relaxed. But by mile 5, as friendly as these new buddies were, I knew I couldn't stay with them much longer. As incredible as it seemed to me, and still does now, I was slightly faster than they were. My knees and shins were aching from shortening my stride, and I knew that if I was going to finish this race in a reasonable amount of time with my dignity intact, I needed to stick to my established training pace. Now what was I supposed to do? I couldn't just randomly run off without an explanation. Even if I did, I was only slightly faster than they were, meaning I'd be only a few awkward feet in front of them for the next mile or two. I spent the next two miles attempting to figure out how I could ditch these two lovely ladies without seeming excessively rude. My salvation came in the form of a full bladder.

"I really need to go to the bathroom," one of the ladies said. "All that coffee this morning."

"I'll go with you," the other said. I looked over at the portable toilet she pointed to over on the sidewalk. The line was at least fifteen people deep. It would be a minimum of thirty minutes before they'd be back in the race. There was no way I could stay with them. If I stopped, I might never start again.

"Hey, guys, it's been great running with you, but I need to keep going. I'll see you at the finish?"

"For sure!" they said. "Nice meeting you, and good luck!"

And just like that, at mile 7 of the 26.2-mile marathon, I found myself alone. This was exactly what I had feared would happen, and here I was, smack in the middle of my marathon nightmare. In an attempt to convince myself that things weren't as bad as they might seem, I took a deep breath, then peeled off my windbreaker and tied it around my waist. I rolled my shoulders back and gave myself a little pep talk as I jogged on.

You can do this. You've trained hard enough. It stinks that you're alone, but nothing you can do about that now. Remember, Drew's waiting for you at the finish, and he's tracking your split times, so let's keep up the pace. Remember, your goal is to simply finish with your dignity intact. You can do it!

Drew was working the race as a member of the medical support team. He was stationed in the medical tent just past the finish line, giving out ice packs for shin splints and putting IVs into the dangerously dehydrated. He signed up for the text alerts that sent him a message every time I crossed a mile marker.

"I'll be keeping track of your progress, and when I get the text saying you've finished, I'll come find you," he'd promised. I appreciated that he said "when," not "if." As much as I wanted a respectable time for myself, I wanted to impress Drew even more.

The next eight miles went by in a blur. Run, drink, run, drink. *Try not to think about your legs. Try not to think about your feet. Read the funny signs that spectators are holding up. Smile at the kids waving flags. Enjoy the beautiful Washington, DC, scenery and the fall leaves. Whatever you do, don't think about how far you still have to go.* Mile 13. Mile 14. Mile 15. I had just turned a corner near the National Mall, close to the Washington Monument, when I heard someone calling my name. I swiveled my head and saw my best friends and neighbors, Jennifer and Amber, up ahead. They knew I was running the marathon and wanted to support me however they could. So they'd thrown a few of their kids into Jennifer's minivan and driven across the river from our nearby Fort Belvoir, and there they were, chanting my name, holding up two big, happy signs. One said, GO Stacey GO!; the other, NO ONE MADE YOU DO THIS. I ran toward them, thrilled to have my own tiny fan club, but terrified that if I slowed my pace at all, I'd never get it back.

"Thank you for coming!" I yelled as I ran by.

"You look great! Good job! Keep going!" they shouted back.

I jogged on, their surprise appearance boosting my energy. As I ran, I thought about what good friends they were. *How did they figure out where to stand so they would see me? How did they know when I would be running by? I hope they didn't have to wait too long. And when did they have time to make those signs? Finding a parking spot must have been a nightmare. Gosh, I hope they didn't have to pay for parking. Such good friends. That was so nice of them. I need to remember to thank them tomorrow. I'm sure they're headed home now. I hope the traffic isn't too bad. I wonder which bridge they'll take back over the river.* For another few miles my mind stayed occupied thinking about my thoughtful friends and their travel logistics. Mile 17. Mile 18. Mile 19.

Just after mile 20, I started to feel it in my legs. I could feel myself slowing down. Mile 21. Julie and I hadn't run much farther than this in our training sessions, and soon I would have run farther than I ever had in my life, a big mental hurdle. Every so often I passed a runner limping along the side of the road or sitting down on the grass, waiting for an ambulance to pick them up. The spectators were fewer in this back section of the race. As we circled around the Tidal Basin, the colorful autumn leaves that had fallen from the cherry blossom trees arching above us muffled the sounds of our pounding feet. The side of my knee started to ache, a new injury that had developed over the last few weeks of training.

Oh man, I thought to myself, *I can't believe I still have five miles to go. That's almost twice a 5K distance . . . I think?* After I'd been running for almost four hours, accurate math was beyond my remaining brain power. I passed a fit-looking guy hobbling along the side of the road at a slow walk. *Look at him walking,* I began to reason with myself. *I could walk right now too, and no one would know. It would feel pretty awesome to walk for a mile or two. My hips are so stiff. I can't feel my feet. My legs hurt. I don't know if I'm going to make it to the finish. It's just too far.*

Not long after, I passed a young woman in cute athletic clothes sitting on the curb. She was rubbing her ankle and grimacing as she twirled her foot around. *Oh man, poor her. She makes it all the way to mile 21 and then she twists her ankle. When her friends ask, "How was the race?" she'll probably be like, "Well, I was about to win the entire thing when, wouldn't you know it, I twisted my ankle!" Then her friends will give her big hugs and tell her that the important thing was that she tried and that she's still their hero. So she'll get all the accolades for doing her best without having to take one more painful step. That actually sounds pretty great. You know, I could fake an ankle injury right now and no one would be the wiser. I could just sit on the curb and wait for the medics to come scoop me up, just like she is. Then I wouldn't have to finish the race, but people won't think I'm a quitter. What's the big deal about running a marathon anyway? That lady isn't going to finish, and she doesn't look too disappointed. And what about that guy who was limping earlier? There's no way he's going to finish. Yeah, I think a fake injury is just the ticket. Let's see, if I wanted to act like I twisted my ankle, how would I do it? I would need to be convincing, but I wouldn't want to be overly dramatic about it. Maybe a fake cramp instead? Or a pulled muscle? Hamstring? Calf muscle? What's most believable?* I was completely overanalyzing how to fake an injury and, to my own ears, sounding pretty darn reasonable. I just wanted the race to be over. I just wanted the pain to end. I had hit the wall.

✳ ✳ ✳

In this race we call life it's not a matter of *if* you will hit the wall but *when*. We are broken people living in a broken world where hardship and strife are as certain as death and taxes. We are not superhumans or robots who can get knocked down over and over again without missing a beat. If you can honestly say you've never hit a wall in your life, just wait five minutes. It's coming.

The walls most of us encounter are not the type of physical exhaustion we hit while running an actual marathon; they are emotional, mental, and spiritual walls that are a shared piece of the human experience. And because these intangible walls live in our mind, heart, and soul, they can be far harder to break through than physical ones. For a little while you can convince yourself to do anything, to endure anything. Picture the unexpected bursts of physical strength that make the news—a mom who lifts a car off an injured child or the prisoner of war who endures torture for years but never gives up hope. Usually when we hit walls, it's not the physical pain that forces us to stop, it's the voice in our head that begs us to quit, walk away, or crawl under our blankets and never come out again. That voice convinces us to stop trying, to stop caring, or to fake an injury by whispering one big lie into our ears: *Life will always feel like this.*

When we hit an impasse, it feels like nothing will ever change. I've felt the pain of slamming into the wall many times. The familiar feeling came from attending funeral after funeral for fellow soldiers; struggling through a never-ending string of emotionally draining days while parenting solo; or being trapped in my house during a global pandemic with no vaccine in sight. I've seen friends hit the wall when yet another round of IVF failed, a relationship crumbled, a business closed, the cancer spread, or a child stormed out in anger. Sometimes it can seem as if life is just a series of walls lined up like dominoes in front of us. If we manage to make it over the first, we may reason, there are just more and more to come, so maybe we should just give up.

That voice in our head tells us that life will always feel this hard, that our days will always be this dark, that this pain will never go away, or that the people in our lives will always disappoint us. Our natural human tendency is to accept that lie because in the moment, everything we think and feel tells us it's true. Discouraged, we drop our heads and look down, shoulders hunched, staring at our own feet as we attempt to plod along alone. We reach within ourselves for strength to endure, and when we come up empty, we cry out, "I can't do this anymore!" The world tells us that we have the right to get angry or go numb. We lash out, reject those who want to help us, and rail against the circumstances that brought us to this point. Then we drink or smoke or sleep or eat—whatever it takes to not feel this way anymore. We hit the wall and stick there like a bug on a windshield.

God offers us another option, one that is powerful and effective because it does not depend on our own inner fortitude as the sole source of our energy and strength. The Bible recounts story after story of tired and struggling people hitting wall after wall, but eventually breaking through because of the energy and strength offered through community and a connection to the ultimate source of life and love, God himself. We may not always see it, we may not always feel it, but nevertheless, it is always there: "Now faith is confidence in what we hope for and assurance about what we do not see" (Hebrews 11:1).

The way I see it, faith is the belief that despite what the voice in your head is telling you, you can, and will, break through that wall. It's a willingness to surrender your own attempts to do it alone and instead say to God, "I don't know how, I don't know when, but I trust you when you say you will give me the strength I need for today. I have an expectant hope that you will eventually help me break through this wall and that there are better days on the other side."

It may not be easy. In fact, it probably won't be. In my experience, faith requires a willingness to fight and a level of grittiness and spunk I don't often tap into. And by the time you get on the other side of the wall, you often aren't looking too pretty. You are far more likely to be bloody, sweaty, dirty, and heaving than you are to be clean and serene. God never promised us an easy life. In fact, he promises us

needed it for my fake ankle sprain tumble. My head drooped and I shuffled along, staring at the pavement six inches in front of the toes of my sneakers.

"Stacey! Hey! You're doing it! You're doing it! You're going to make it!"

My head snapped up. I recognized those voices. There, just behind the flag, stood Jennifer and Amber. Jumping up and down, they were cheering and smiling, waving their arms and the signs over their heads like they were witnessing a historic Olympic finish. I assumed they had headed home an hour ago, but there they were, still cheering. Seeing them brought tears to my eyes. I'd never been more thankful for enthusiastic and obnoxiously loud friends. Their electricity and confidence in my ability to finish the race were contagious, and I felt my energy level surge back up. I ran over, as thrilled to see them as they were to see me.

"I'm doing it, you guys! I'm going to make it to the finish! I'm doing it!"

"Yes!" they screamed, jumping up and down, as excited for me as if they were running the race themselves. "You are doing it!" They walked alongside me down the street, easily keeping up with my snail's pace.

I pulled the windbreaker from around my waist and shoved it into Amber's hands.

"Could you take this home for me? I can't wear it the rest of the way." I felt the need to shed something—anything—in order to keep moving forward. Amber laughed, as my tone implied my one-ounce windbreaker fluttering around my waist had been the equivalent of wearing a lead vest this entire race.

"Yes, yes! Go, go, go! We'll see you at home! You're doing it!" They continued to cheer as I jogged off, their unexpected appearance giving me new life. Taking off my jacket made me feel sleek and unencumbered, like a boxer taking off his robe before a fight. I looked at the other spectators lined up on the curb, clapping and waving. They believed I could finish this race. Amber and Jennifer believed I could finish this race. Drew believed I could finish this race. I needed to believe it too. The pain in my hips, legs, and feet remained, but a fist of determination tightened within me and punched through the wall.

I ran the last four miles physically hurting but mentally light and nimble, thinking about my friends' confidence in me and Drew waiting for me at the finish. I wasn't breaking any speed records. In fact, I'm pretty sure I saw a guy on crutches pass me on my left, but I kept moving forward. As I ran, I thought about how great it would feel to say I was a race finisher and to show my kids the big, shiny medal on its long, brightly colored ribbon. I thought about how I'd be able to look back on this day and know I'd survived, pushing myself harder and farther than I ever had before. I thought about how from this day forward, any race I ran would seem short and easy by comparison. Then I thought about how good it was going to feel to take a long, hot shower at home, followed by a long, deep nap.

Up ahead, I could see the finish line, the big inflatable arch stretching across the road adjacent to the Iwo Jima Memorial. In the last five hundred yards, the crowds grew dense and the cheering bloomed into a deafening roar. Strangers read the front of my sweaty shirt and yelled my name. I leaned forward, pumping my arms to drive myself up the last hill and across the pad that would record my finish time. I crossed the painted line and stumbled forward, my legs stiff and my feet numb. It was finally over. I'd done it. A young, handsome Marine hung my heavy finisher's medal around my salt-encrusted neck; another handed me a cold bottle of water and a thermal blanket. I blindly followed the rest of the finishers toward the recovery area like a sheep, my feet moving with a mind of their own. The fenced pathway opened into a green lawn where dozens of fellow finishers wandered around in a daze, just like me. Drew popped out of the crowd in his bright yellow medical team shirt, his stethoscope around his neck, just as he promised he would.

"You did it!" he said. "I knew you could do it!" Seeing his proud smile and settling into his warm hug pushed me over the edge. I began to cry, overcome by the enormity of what I had just accomplished.

"I did it," I said. "I don't feel so great, but I did it. I finished." Then I dropped to the ground and lay on the grass for several minutes before standing up and heading home for that long, hot shower.

✳ ✳ ✳

At the mission midpoint, Drew and I know we've both hit the wall. We aren't surprised or even overly worried or insecure about it. Having broken through enough walls in life, we know it is temporary and we have faith we will eventually come out on the other side. But experience has taught us that we can shorten the impasse if we proactively fight through it rather than try to wait it out. So we share with our small group that we are struggling, and they pray for us regularly. We talk about our feelings with each other and the crew psychologist. I reach out to my family and friends for hope and companionship. Drew makes more phone calls to friends and family on their birthdays or just to check in.

On January 10, 2020, we finally allow ourselves to begin counting down the days until Drew's return. Before that, the number of days before our reunion was so high it only made us depressed. But this day marks one hundred days until landing, which is a much more reasonable and countable number. The kids and I cut out one hundred blue and gold squares from cardstock and punch a hole in the corner of each one. Amelia uses her best fancy lettering skills to label each paper square one to one hundred. Then we string them up on the chandelier over our kitchen table so we can remove one square each day. Every day when Drew calls, we tell him how many days are left until he comes home. Then he and I brainstorm ideas about where we should vacation the following summer and what we are looking forward to most about the days when we will be together again.

One day, we wake up and realize our fog has lifted. We've broken through the wall.

"We're doing it," Drew tells me. "We're doing it!"

"Yes," I say. "As impossible as it seemed a few months ago, we're doing it. The finish line is just around the corner. We're doing it!"

CHAPTER 9

REUNION

ACCEPT THAT LIFE IS BOTH HARD AND GOOD

When the astronauts returned home from their historic first landing on the moon in 1969, NASA took countless precautions to safeguard the general population from potentially dangerous alien lunar microorganisms that might have hitched a ride back to Earth. As the *Apollo 11*'s charred command module *Columbia* bobbed in the Pacific Ocean, Navy rescue divers in full scuba gear opened the hatch and handed the astronauts specialized hazmat suits known as biological isolation garments. Somehow the astronauts had to zip themselves into these full-body containment suits, complete with gloves and gas mask, while still inside the tiny bobbing capsule. When the crew eventually climbed out of the capsule and into the rubber rescue raft, they were sprayed down with disinfectant, just in case.

And the precautions were only beginning. One by one, Navy sailors then hoisted the astronauts into a helicopter, which flew them to the USS *Hornet*, the Navy ship tasked with recovering the crew and capsule and returning them to port in Hawaii. When it landed on the USS *Hornet*'s deck, the helicopter—with the entire crew still inside—was lowered below deck. From there it was towed closer to the Mobile Quarantine Facility, a retrofitted Airstream vacation trailer parked on the ship. Astronauts Collins, Armstrong, and Aldrin walked the ten steps from the helicopter into the trailer where, along with a NASA physician and engineer, they stayed until the ship docked in Hawaii two days later. Once in port, a crane hoisted the trailer, with the crew inside, off the Navy ship and onto the back of a flatbed truck, which drove them to nearby Hickam Air Force Base, where personnel loaded the trailer, with the crew still inside, into the belly of a waiting C-141 cargo plane. The Air Force plane then flew eight hours to Ellington Field, located adjacent to NASA in Houston. Once there, the trailer, with the crew still inside, was hoisted by a crane onto the back of another flatbed truck and driven to the Lunar Receiving Laboratory, located in what is now Johnson Space Center. The crew remained in quarantine for another two weeks before being allowed to return home to their families.

In hindsight, those elaborate safety precautions seem excessive and almost quaint. We can chuckle at photos of those three American heroes peeking through the back window of their Airstream trailer like a trio of brothers stuck on an endless family RV vacation. But in 1969, scientists didn't know what they didn't know. Because they imagined the possibility of dangerous "moon germs" spreading across the globe, they took the precautions deemed necessary to protect the human race. For most of my life, that story was nothing but a fascinating history lesson. When I worked at the National Air and Space Museum in Washington, DC, as a college student, I walked past the *Columbia* command module several times a day. Every so often I'd peek in the open hatch and marvel at the astronauts' ability to fit themselves into such tight quarters. Years later, Drew and I took our kids to the National Air and Space Museum's Steven F. Udvar-Hazy Center in Chantilly, Virginia, where we walked around the *Apollo 11* Mobile Quarantine Facility and pointed at the trailer window we recognized from those famous photographs while the kids whined and pulled our arms, trying to steer us toward the gift shop. But in April 2020, that charming historical event took on a much more personal meaning.

* * *

As COVID-19 continues to spread across the planet and Drew's landing date creeps closer, we begin to realize that his return to Earth will probably not follow the usual pattern. Most Soyuz landings follow the same time-tested and reliable routine. The capsule lands under parachute in the flat, desert steppe of Kazakhstan. Recovery crews consisting of Russian, American, and other international partners descend on the landing site within minutes, and the three-person crew is physically pulled out of the cramped capsule by their arms and into the sun for the first time in months. Multiple high-definition cameras capture all the action, beginning when the capsule breaks through the Earth's atmosphere and continuing up close with the crew and their support teams once they land on the ground. After being lowered into special chairs, each member of the crew has their helmet and gloves removed for a quick medical check. Nearby, the science team sets up a sizable field tent. Each astronaut and cosmonaut has a turn with a satellite phone to call their loved ones before they are carried into the tent for the removal of their space suit, a quick cleanup, and a few more rounds of medical tests. They are then carried in their chairs to a waiting all-terrain vehicle that drives them the short distance to the waiting Russian helicopters, one for each crew member. The helicopters fly to an airfield where the NASA jet is waiting to whisk the American astronauts back to Texas. The jet touches down at Ellington Field, and only twenty-four hours after landing on Earth, the astronauts walk off the plane to greet their jubilant friends and family. They spend a night or two in the quarantine facility at Johnson Space Center so NASA scientists can collect time-sensitive human data, and that's it. Often less than forty-eight hours after floating in space, American astronauts can be back in their own houses, sleeping in their own beds.

Under normal circumstances, the return is pretty straightforward and quick. Some astronaut families watch the landing from home and invite dozens of people to celebrate with them, while others choose to watch from mission control with a smaller group of friends and family. Either way, the astronaut families, along with a gaggle of fellow astronauts, are waiting on the tarmac when the NASA jet lands at Ellington Field.

For most of his mission, we expect Drew's return to follow the normal pattern. He and his American crewmate Jessica will return to Texas so quickly that the kids and I will stay home to watch their return to Earth. But then COVID-19 happens, and the usual Soyuz landing routine unravels. At home, everything shuts down. Like everyone else, the kids and I scramble to adjust to virtual learning, and I bust out my sewing machine to start making face masks. My coworkers and I schedule Zoom meetings to discuss the reshuffling of organizational priorities, while secretly peeking over each other's virtual shoulders for a rare glimpse into each other's homes. Each night when I talk to Drew, I describe the newest and strangest aspects of the COVID world he will soon return to.

For the first time, my summaries of the previous day are more novel than his. "I snuck a peek at Gabby's class Zoom meeting today," I tell him, "and it was pretty much all twenty kids trying to hold their pets up in front of the computer screen and talk at the same time. These teachers are not paid enough.

"I switched to the grocery pickup where they just load everything into your car. It's pretty great. Only I asked for one bunch of bananas and instead they gave me one banana. What kind of weirdo orders a single banana?

"All this sitting in front of my computer for work and school stuff is killing my backside. I had no choice but to order a special cushion to support my apparently sensitive tailbone, so congrats! You're officially married to an old lady.

"I saw a woman at the store today wearing a homemade hazmat suit made of trash bags and duct tape. Things are getting weird down here. Maybe you should stay in space a little bit longer."

Meanwhile, less than ten miles away, NASA closes their doors to all but essential personnel, shifting to a virtual workplace while the decision-makers and doctors scramble to make sense of what the pandemic means for a returning crew and their families. One thing is certain, nothing will be the same. Exactly two weeks before Drew's landing date, I receive a phone call from the crew physician.

"If you and the kids want to be able to see Drew after he lands, you'll need to go into full quarantine," he tells me. "You can't go anywhere. No grocery stores, no nothing."

"Okay," I say. All of the schools, gyms, churches, offices, and most stores are already closed, so this isn't a huge change of plans. "Starting when?"

"Starting now," he tells me. "And you need to take everyone's temperatures twice a day."

So the kids and I lock ourselves in the house, leaving only to take socially distanced jogs or bike rides around the neighborhood. Luckily, I'd seen something like this coming and had stocked up on essentials the week before, so we aren't reduced to eating tuna fish or drinking powdered milk. Whenever we do need something, friends pick it up and leave it on our front doorstep. The kids and I hunker down like polar bears in a blizzard, watching movies and finishing jigsaw puzzles. Twice a day, I chase them around the house with my thermometer and clipboard, recording their temperatures on my spreadsheet while shoving another gummy vitamin into their mouths. When they complain, I remind them of how serious the situation is.

"Quit complaining, you guys," I say while I click my pen and fill in another row on my temperature chart. "Your father spacewalked for over forty-five hours and orbited the Earth 4,300 times. The least you can do is take your vitamin. Now open up."

Meanwhile, the crew receives daily updates on the ISS about how the global shutdown is throwing wrenches into every aspect of the usual landing routine. Almost every night Drew shares a new update or tweak to the plan.

"So here's the latest," he tells me only a few days before landing. "After the capsule hits the ground, the usual number of support people on site will be cut dramatically. Those who are there will be wearing gloves, masks, and who knows what other layers of protective gear. They will take us directly to the helicopters, no medical tent. And because of all the airport shutdowns, even in Kazakhstan, the NASA jet can't fly to the usual airfield; it will have to land at one much farther away. So after a three-hour helicopter ride, we will be loaded into three separate medical vans, where we will be driven for another three hours to the airport where the jet is waiting. And then we'll fly home to Ellington with one refueling stop along the way. And once we get back to NASA, they'll keep us in the quarantine facility for a week."

"A week?" I say. "That's way longer than usual! Do you think they will let us come visit you?" The idea that Drew could be back on the planet, less than thirty minutes away from us, and yet we might not be able to see or touch him after all this time was unfathomable.

"I hope so, so keep up the strict quarantine just in case. This could all change tomorrow." Drew is far more tolerant of the constant shifting of plans and restrictions than I am. Of course, he isn't trapped in a house with four bored kids, and the view out his window is far more interesting than mine.

As predicted, our plans change on an almost daily basis. I begin to dread when my phone rings and I see one of my NASA contacts on the caller ID. They never call to tell me that the restrictions have been relaxed or that things are getting simpler. The final plan is a mixture of good and bad news. The good news is that the kids and I will be allowed to watch the landing at mission control, be at Ellington when the NASA jet lands, and stay with Drew for the first few days of his weeklong quarantine. The bad news is that in order to be allowed such close contact with the crew, we need to keep our strict quarantine in place before, during, and after they land. That means that whether we watch the landing from home or at mission control, the kids and I will be alone—no friends or family allowed. Only my NASA chaperone and the same astronaut escort from the launch can join us, and only because they are in quarantine themselves. In other words, our crew of five is just as isolated as the crew of three about to return from space. Not exactly what we imagined when we fantasized about Drew's return during all these long months away. As the return plans become more complicated, it starts to feel more and more like the *Apollo 11* return, except that instead of protecting the community from the crew, we are protecting the crew from the community. Drew and his two crewmates are literally the only three people who have not yet been touched by COVID, and NASA isn't about to let it happen on their watch.

The landing is scheduled for just after midnight on April 17. It is no use trying to take a nap beforehand, so the kids and I stay up, watching movies and eating Mexican food to pass the time. Even though we are not allowed to have guests with us, I chose to watch the landing from mission control with the kids; it just seems like an occasion that's too momentous to experience alone in our own living room. We arrive at mission control just after 11 p.m. My astronaut escort and chaperone meet us in the empty parking lot, greeting us from six feet away with their face masks on.

"Hey, everyone! How are you doing? Excited to watch your dad's landing tonight?" my escort asks in the dark.

The kids respond with tired smiles before putting on their own masks. We cross the parking lot and make our way into the seemingly abandoned building, entering through a side door. With no guests, no pomp, and no celebration, it feels more like we are the nighttime cleaning crew showing up for our shift than an excited astronaut family come to watch Drew's dramatic landing and the first stage of his journey home. Once in the mission control viewing room, my escort passes around a container of chocolate chip cookies before finding a seat a safe distance behind me. The kids spread out, sprawling out on whatever chair they fall into, a cookie in each hand. Down on the floor of mission control, a handful of NASA engineers gaze at their computer screens or click an occasional button. Soyuz landings are managed from Moscow, so other than the NASA flight controllers listening and following along in case of emergency and the NASA TV coverage of the landing projected onto the big screen, it is business as usual in Houston. The single astronaut and two cosmonauts remaining on board the ISS are still asleep, and the overnight shift at mission control is a skeleton crew. The late hour, the emptiness of the building, and the physical distance required by COVID protocols make the silence in the room even thicker than usual.

"I have to warn you," my escort says, "I don't think the video coverage is going to be as good as it usually is. Thanks to COVID, they restricted the number of people at the landing, including the camera crews. I don't think they have the usual high-definition cameras, and I don't think they'll be able to film from the rescue helicopters like they usually do, so we may not see any live coverage until they land on the ground."

"We won't?" I ask. Without the live shots of the tiny, burnt capsule swinging under the massive red-and-white-striped parachutes, I wonder how we'll know when the capsule lands safely back on the Earth. We've been at mission control only twenty minutes, and I am already a little disappointed. Our chaperone flips on the wall-mounted TV, and the voice of NASA's narrator fills the room. I pull out my printed copy of the landing timeline, which includes a minute-by-minute breakdown of every reentry stage and checkpoint for the capsule. Essentially unchanged since the 1960s, the Soyuz landing timeline is precise and predictable down to the second.

I glance at my watch and then back to the paper in my hand. In exactly one minute, at 11:22 p.m., the Soyuz engines should fire for a de-orbit burn, a firing of the main engine to slow down the spacecraft and drop it back toward the Earth. Like clockwork, a minute later, the narrator confirms the successful burn. Now there is nothing to do but wait.

According to my timeline, over the course of the next thirty minutes, the Soyuz spacecraft will separate into two parts, the orbital module and the command module. The orbital module will drift off and eventually burn up in the Earth's atmosphere like a large piece of space trash. The command module, with Drew and his two crewmates inside, in contrast, should blast through the Earth's atmosphere at over 2,000 miles per hour. The air friction will cause the outer, protective layers of the capsule to burn off, and the extreme heat will create a temporary communications blackout between the crew and the ground.

It's a long and boring half hour. As the minutes tick by, there's nothing to see, nothing on the screen to help track the landing progress. The television coverage flips between a generic blank map of Kazakhstan and headshots of the crew taken the year before.

"Get your feet off the back of the seats," I scold the kids. "This isn't our living room."

You can't blame them for wanting to put their feet up, I mentally admonish myself. *So far, with the exception of the cookies, watching this landing has all the excitement of hanging out in a dentist's office waiting room. It's late, and all this sitting around with nothing to see is making me cranky.*

This is all wrong, I think to myself as my inner dissident climbs up on its soapbox. *I should have a raucous circle of friends surrounding me. We should be laughing and talking while they pat me on the back and congratulate me for holding down the home front for nine long months.* Exhaling sharply through my nose, I look down at my paper again. By this point, we should be looking up at the screens, enjoying the breathtaking, high-definition coverage of the gumdrop-shaped capsule swinging under its softly pulsating parachutes, gently falling to Earth at a leisurely 15 mph. Just a second before it hits the Earth, as the cameras pan in, we would expect to see a blast of smoke and dirt as small retro-rockets under the capsule fire in an attempt to cushion the impact. Then we should be erupting in cheers and jubilation, knowing that the crew is safely back on Earth. This room should be bursting at the seams with euphoric, high-fiving family members in NASA T-shirts while I hand out mission-themed swag, such as buttons and patches, as we toast Drew's safe return.

This should be a party, but it feels more like a wake, my inner monologue complains. This intangible loss sparks a low level of anger that simmers in my gut as we sit in silence, waiting for any word from the narrator. With no video feed from the helicopters, she is as blind to the landing progress as we are. The screen continues to flip wordlessly between the maddeningly blank map and the crew photos. I'm miffed that this is so boring. I'm disappointed that my friends can't be with me. I'm annoyed that the kids keep asking me innocent questions like "Why is this taking so long?" "Where is Daddy now?" and "Why aren't the cameras showing us anything?" I'm resentful that this is one more thing that COVID has taken away from me, from my kids, and from Drew's parents watching the coverage in their living room instead of here with me.

As the silent minutes tick by, my irritation begins to morph into concern. The capsule should be on the ground by now. A chair squeaks behind me as my escort shifts in his seat. "I'm sure they're on the ground now and fine," he says to me in an attempt to be reassuring.

"Uh-huh," I say, wishing his blind faith made me feel more optimistic. I roll my head in a circle, trying to loosen the tension gathering at the base of my neck. Without realizing it, I've been tensing up my shoulders with each passing minute. I'd rather the kids think I'm bored or tired rather than worried or upset, so I roll my shoulders back and rest my head in my hand as if I'm waiting for my number to be called at the DMV. Inside, my mind is flipping through cue cards covered in questions.

Why haven't the recovery teams reported seeing the parachutes? Is there a problem with the parachutes? Is something else wrong? Can they not locate the capsule? It's not unheard of for a capsule to land somewhere slightly off course from the landing target. *Is that what's happening here? Or has something really terrible happened and they are trying to contain the bad news until they have more details?* If the capsule re-enters the Earth's atmosphere just a few degrees off from the correct orientation, it could be catastrophic. If the capsule isn't slowed down enough by the parachutes or retro-rockets, the crew could be seriously injured or killed on impact.

With no information, my overactive imagination shifts into overdrive, and a balloon of anxiety inflates in my chest. I sit forward in my chair and shove the paper back in my pocket—we've now been off the timeline for what feels like a lifetime. A prick of panic tickles my spine. I've never needed a comforting hug more than I do at this moment. I turn to look at my teenage son a few seats away, and his blank expression makes it clear there are no hugs coming from that direction. Two rows up, the girls are playing with the chaperone's laptop and eating more cookies, oblivious to my mild distress. Pandemic protocols and my own pride make it impossible for me to turn to my escort and ask, "Can I have a hug?" or for him to offer any comforting pats on my back or reassuring hand squeezes. There may be several people with me in the room, but I feel alone.

A quick statement from the narrator breaks through the silence.

"And we have confirmed landing of the crew at approximately 12:16 a.m. central time; 1:16 a.m. eastern time, and 11:16 a.m. Kazakhstan time, almost five hours after sunrise at the landing site.

Jessica Meir, Oleg Skripochka, and Drew Morgan have returned. The vehicle has been reported by the Russian search and recovery forces to be on its side."

With those two flat sentences, the worst is over. The kids' heads snap toward me, looking to my reaction as a gauge for their own. I give them all a comforting smile, and they reflexively smile back in return, turning their attention back to the TV screen. The capsule is on the ground. I should feel relief and joy. But with no visual confirmation, the balloon in my chest remains. We should be cheering, we should be hugging, we should be crying happy tears. Instead, I stare at the TV in silence, waiting for proof. My inner skeptic springs up and demands action. *Just give me a quick visual of the capsule, of the crew, of the helicopters, of anything!* she screams in my head. *Get your crap together, camera crew! You're killing us over here!* Outwardly, I keep my mouth shut, frozen in a flat smile while I nervously pick at my fingernails.

A little Soyuz capsule icon pops onto the blank map, presumably to indicate the general vicinity of where they landed. It tells me nothing I don't already know, and at this point, the graphic almost feels like an insult. I feel more in the dark and disconnected from what is going on than I have at any other moment in the mission. It's exasperating and disconcerting at the same time.

It takes another twenty minutes for the camera crew to arrive at the landing site. By the time the blurry, pixelated picture flashes onto the screen, the capsule's hatch is already open and the rescue team is actively pulling Oleg out into the open air. Jessica is removed next. Drew is taken out last. As I catch my first glimpse of him, I audibly gasp. I expected him to look tired from the long day. I knew that his skin would be pale after not seeing the sun for nine months and that he'd probably look a little sick from the jarring descent. I was not fully prepared for what I see: Drew doesn't look like himself. He is not the robust, healthy man I've known for twenty-five years and with whom I had a video conference just a couple of days ago. Space travel has propelled Drew into the future, and he looks eighty-five years old. He isn't pale; he is gray. He doesn't look tired; he looks ancient. He gives the camera a forced smile and waves as they carry him to his chair. As the camera pans to get a closer look at the newly emerged crew, I see him for only a minute before his support team surrounds him, blocking him from the camera's view. The terrible quality of the picture makes the coverage seem like a replay of a Soyuz landing from thirty years ago. Had I not personally known those blurry, pixelated faces, I might be tempted to believe they're not real. Any relief I may have felt seeing the capsule safely on the ground has now been replaced with concern for Drew's well-being. He looks dreadful. *What is wrong with him? Why does he look so sick?* Did those extra three months in space really make that much of a difference? How is he ever going to survive the long helicopter flight, jostling drive in the van, and detoured plane ride home? *He's going to be miserable. I feel miserable just thinking about it.*

My phone buzzes in my pocket. The number is from the satellite phone they've given Drew to call me.

"Drew? Hello?" I say.

"Stace, hi, it's me." Drew's voice sounds strange and strained. Like he's actively sick but is trying hard to fake feeling upbeat.

"Are you okay? You don't look so good." This is the biggest understatement I have ever made in my entire life.

"Yes, I feel fine. I'm fine. I can only talk for a second."

"Are you *sure* you're fine?" Though I don't say it, it would be more accurate for me to tell him, "You look like a corpse."

"Yes, I'm sure! I'm fine. I'm fine. I have to go now." Why does he keep saying he's fine? Is he trying to reassure me or himself that he's fine? He sure doesn't look or sound "fine" to me. I'm not buying it, but I have to trust he's in good hands.

"Okay, we love you, and we'll see you soon." *If you survive the trip home.*

"Yes, I love you guys. I'll see you soon. Goodbye."

As I hang up and slide my phone back into my purse, I watch the landing team pick Drew up in his chair and carry him out of the camera's view, toward the vehicle which will take them to the helicopter. The video feed ends shortly thereafter, and the TV screen flips to the default NASA logo shown between scheduled programming.

Is that it? I assumed watching the landing would make me emotional, so the day before I stuffed a pack of tissues in my purse. Just thinking about Drew's imminent return brought me to tears several times over the previous few days. But here in the moment, instead of crying from happiness, I want to scream in my grief for the loss of the communal, joyous moment COVID has robbed me of. Like so many other things during the pandemic, the standard event is canceled and its hollow replacement is an utter letdown. I feel detached and disappointed in both the landing coverage and my own lack of emotional reaction. This simply isn't how this was supposed to go. At the same time, I know that in the big picture of things, I've got nothing to complain about. Drew is safely back on Earth. He will soon be home with us again. I should be thankful and grateful for the moment I do have, not emotionally distant or disgruntled by what I don't. My head knows this, but my heart is having a hard time letting go. I feel guilty that I'm even wrestling with these conflicting feelings.

My chaperone and escort stand up, signaling that the landing program is over. It's 1 a.m., time to go home. My escort walks us back to our car in the vacant parking lot, and my phone buzzes endlessly as friends and family text their congratulations. I don't know if it's the early hour, the large coffee I drank earlier to stay awake, or just pent-up emotions, but as I climb into the driver's seat, I feel nauseated. My head hurts. I wish I could cry just to have a little emotional release, but my eyes are bone dry. By the time I pull back into our driveway twenty minutes later, I just want to go to sleep.

"Put yourselves to bed," I say to the kids as I walk into my bedroom and shut the door. I fall into bed, thinking about the previous few hours. Is Drew really back? It seems impossible. The video coverage was just blurry enough that it didn't seem 100 percent legit. He's been gone for so long, the idea of him coming back home and sleeping in this bed again feels foreign and uncomfortable. I am so happy to have him back safely, and yet when I think of the gray face of the man they pulled out of that capsule, the full weight of our upcoming reunion settles on my chest like a baby elephant. Lying in the dark, my thoughts and feelings tumble within me, just as they did in Baikonur 272 days earlier. I am no longer alone. Life as we know it will be different once again for our family. I eventually drift off, thinking about Drew's long journey home and wondering what in the world is going to come next.

✳ ✳ ✳

In the last few weeks before Drew's return, countless well-meaning friends and strangers ask if the kids and I are excited about Drew coming home. "Of course we are!" I tell them. I love Drew and the kids love their father. I miss my best friend and am lonely without him. But as any military spouse will tell you, reunions are complex, full of messy interactions and weird readjustments. You don't really "get excited" for awkward transitions. So *excited* isn't really the right word for what I am feeling. I'm not sure what the right word is, but it is far more nuanced than that. What seems like a simple question doesn't have a simple answer, but I'm not about to stand in the grocery store cereal aisle and attempt to explain the deep psychology behind my tangle of emotions. So in order to let us both get on with our lives as quickly as possible, I smile and give my sincere but one-dimensional answer.

These types of questions are nothing new. Throughout the mission I have often been asked well-meaning and seemingly simple questions, to which I usually gave an equally simple and well-meaning answer.

"Isn't it so crazy to think that Drew is *in space*?"
"Yes. So crazy."

"Is Drew having a blast up there?"
"Yes, he's having a great time."

"What do the kids think of their dad being in space?"
"They're excited."

"You doing okay?"
"We're great, thanks."

Most people aren't really looking for my full-color, multidimensional answer when they toss me those softball questions. When someone is just making polite conversation, do they really want me to wax philosophical about my fears while their ice cream melts in the shopping cart? Of course not! It's better for both of us if I say, "Fine, thanks," and we both move on with our lives, unencumbered by deep life reflection. The danger is that over time, clean and one-dimensional answers can begin to erode others' perception of our family's unabridged, complex reality.

One-dimensional thinking encourages us to sort life experiences into one of two categories: good or bad. Life is either fantastic or it is terrible. If social media is any reflection of our own internal dialogue, looking back it's clear I'm a card-carrying member of Team Fantastic. Members of Team Fantastic are most often found online, curating their pictures and captions to portray a life without struggle or strain. *Everything is great! My kids are great! My marriage is great! My work is great! I've never been happier! Rainbows! Unicorns! Skittles falling from the sky! Life is one long amazing trip to Cabo!*

While I've never been one to straight-up lie about my reality, I will readily admit to heavily curating what I share with others to maintain the facade that everything is awesome. Scrolling through my Facebook memories, most of my early posts seem to lean heavily on random commentary about reality TV dance competitions or that day's weather. One would think my top concern as a young mom was which celebrities would make it through to the *Dancing with the Stars* finale. My life at the time was a far cry from my easy-breezy social media persona. Honest social media posts would have looked something like this:

I love being a mom! But I have to admit, I didn't expect so much crying. The baby does a lot of crying too.

I have no time to do my hair anymore, so I got a perm. I'm sure I'll NEVER regret this decision!

Even though life was tough, I happily joined Team Fantastic and put on my rose-colored glasses. But every so often, their staunch competitor, Team Terrible, made a pitch for me to switch sides.

Team Terrible focuses on the trials and tribulations of life. This team tends to have fewer members, but they are equally vocal online and in real life. For the Eeyores of Team Terrible, life is one long struggle and is never getting better. *My house is a mess! My in-laws hate me! We don't have enough money! This baby weight is never going away! My boss is out to get me! Life is dreadful. Nothing is solid. Doom! Gloom! Dread! We are all losers in this game called life.*

While this level of pessimism runs contrary to my nature, I've been tempted to wallow with Team Terrible more often than I care to admit. When two appliances break in the same week, I'm sure the house is crumbling around me. When a coworker criticizes my work or ignores my email, I'm convinced she hates me. When I fight with Drew or tussle with a friend, I'm resigned to a life alone and unloved. Life is terrible. Full stop.

Whether you are a member of Team Fantastic or Team Terrible, maintaining a singular life narrative requires an exhausting amount of self-editing. While it's natural to swing between the two teams on a regular basis, sometimes even hour to hour, the danger comes when we begin to dig ourselves a permanent foxhole in one camp or the other and fight off anyone or anything that attempts to dislodge us. Over time, we can come to believe that life is either hard or it is good—it cannot be both. Black or white. The truth is, every season of life is a complicated mix of events as well as our reflexive reactions to them, which then create a variety pack of perceptions and emotions. If we accept the possibility that life can be hard and good at the same time, the way we feel about our circumstances—positive or negative—begins to change.

When we first arrived at NASA, I was a starry-eyed astronaut wife. In between unpacking boxes, I read a history of what was once called the Astronaut Wives Club, now the Astronaut Spouses Group. I was blown away by the wives of the early space program. These women bonded together over their shared experiences and adopted the words "Happy, Proud, Thrilled" as their early motto. It was a reference to the phrase the wives often repeated to the press camped outside their homes for the traditional "postlanding" press conference. I loved that motto. As a newly minted astronaut wife, I couldn't imagine being anything but happy, proud, and thrilled when it came to Drew's space career. How could I be anything else? After all, astronauts are heroes. They are some of the smartest and bravest people I know. They do the impossible and then come home to tell us about it. I used the motto liberally because I believed it to be true. I was on Team Fantastic. The more I read about those original wives, the more impressed I became. No matter how hard it was, no matter how unbearable the strain, these amazingly composed astronaut wives never hesitated to step outside the house for a press conference to say those three magic words: "I am happy, proud, and thrilled." Because they were happy, proud, and thrilled, just like I was when Drew became an astronaut. That was and still is true. What I didn't fully understand at the time was that there was more to the story. It wasn't quite as black-and-white as I liked to think it was, and over time, my one-dimensional perception began to evolve.

I have met many of the original astronaut wives and heard their firsthand accounts of those crazy, dangerous, and exciting early years. They spoke freely of the pressure and heartache that existed alongside the drama and adventure of that historic era. At the same time, I watched as more of my own friends' spouses flew into space, and I observed up close what the experience was like for them. And then in 2019, after six years of secondhand accounts, I experienced it for myself. It was only then that I fully understood why most astronaut spouses—from the original Mercury, Gemini, and Apollo wives to the Skylab, Space Shuttle, Soyuz, and new American-crewed-vehicle spouses of today—smirk and wiggle our eyebrows a little when we repeat that early, catchy motto. We are Happy, Proud, and Thrilled. But we are also Worried, Tense, and Fatigued. We are Elated and Amazed as much as we are Frustrated and Overwhelmed. We are all of those things, and acknowledging one does not negate the other. Shooting your spouse into outer space isn't a black-or-white experience. It's neither all good nor all bad, in the same way nothing in life is that simple to categorize. It's the best and it's the worst. It's isolating and it's bonding. It's a burden and it's an opportunity. It's painful and it's powerful. It is the hardest thing our family has ever done, and yet we'd do it again in a heartbeat. Like all meaningful events in life, it's all those things and more—all at the same time. That's something too many of us forget when we're trying to make sense of difficult or unusual seasons of our lives by digging our black-and-white foxholes in Team Fantastic's or Team Terrible's camp. We waste our energy and stunt ourselves when we try to stuff our ever-changing, full-spectrum lives into either box.

The apostle Paul tells us, "We know that in all things God works for the good of those who love him." (Romans 8:28). This verse is often used by Team Terrible to encourage us in hard times and by Team Fantastic to embolden us when things are going well.

Yet the writer of Ecclesiastes offers us a perspective that should make both Team Fantastic and Team Terrible very uncomfortable because it speaks to the duality of life experiences that exist in parallel with God's unchanging goodness.

There is a time for everything,
and a season for every activity under the heavens:

a time to be born and a time to die,
a time to plant and a time to uproot,
a time to kill and a time to heal,
a time to tear down and a time to build,
a time to weep and a time to laugh,
a time to mourn and a time to dance,
a time to scatter stones and a time to gather them,
a time to embrace and a time to refrain from embracing,
a time to search and a time to give up,
a time to keep and a time to throw away,
a time to tear and a time to mend,
a time to be silent and a time to speak,
a time to love and a time to hate,
a time for war and a time for peace.

ECCLESIASTES 3:1-8

If I believe that these Bible passages are equally true, then I have no choice but to tear up my Team Fantastic and Team Terrible membership cards. God uses every aspect of my life experiences, not just the very good and not just the very bad. The full-color, multidimensional life he offers me has failure and victory in equal measure. There is as much power in lament as there is in praise. To waste our time focusing on one or the other is to deny the reality of the wild and wonderful world we live in. God offers us variety, surprise outcomes, and unexpected tears of both joy and pain. God does not ask us to curate our experiences before he uses them.

To take full advantage of what God offers us, let's stop exhausting ourselves trying to make life something it's not. It is neither perfection nor a catastrophe. It is not always happy or easy. It's often messy and hard. But it's still good. Life is meant to be enjoyed, and the contrasts of life can exist in the same space at the same time. It's a gift from God and should be viewed as such, on both good and bad days.

Drew's mission to space included some of the best and worst moments of my life, and I know he would say the same. That season challenged and grew me in ways that made me a stronger, better person at the end of it. Yet the stretching process was often awkward and uncomfortable, and sometimes even painful. Drew's return to Earth was one of the happiest and, at the same time, the most anxiety-provoking events in my life. It was not a one-dimensional experience, either good or bad. While in space, Drew had a unique perspective of the Earth. From above, each orbit around our planet was a swirling, multicolored, multidimensional, ever-changing experience. I would describe his homecoming in similar terms. Attempting to capture its complexity in simple black-and-white terms would be impossible.

When we come with a script we want life to follow, we will find only disappointment. Rather than fighting for one team or the other, I invite you to put down your flag and rest. Today may be fantastic. Tomorrow may be terrible. For all we know, you may experience both before lunch. But God offers us a depth of peace and understanding we can find only when we welcome all of what he allows in this short life.

* * *

The day after Drew's landing is a holding pattern of mindless, time-killing activities. I go for a run and finish another puzzle. The kids watch a movie and eat snacks all day. I change some light bulbs and call my mom. I put Drew's toothbrush and razor back on his side of the bathroom counter. In the late afternoon, I text the doctor traveling back to the States with Drew, hoping for some news:

Just checking in to see if you have a Drew update for me.

He responds right away.

Sure, he was dehydrated but is doing better now. There was a lot happening today. When we finally got a signal, it was 0530 your time and he didn't want to call you that early. Anyway, he's eating a panini now. Want him to call you when he finishes?

What the heck? A panini? I text back:

Sure—but don't rush the panini.

Drew calls a couple of hours later from their refueling stop. He has only a few minutes before they have to get back on the plane. In this weird COVID world, the airport will only let them get off the plane on the tarmac and walk around outside for a few minutes before reboarding the plane and taking off again.

"I wasn't feeling so good after landing, so the doc gave me some nausea medication. I really don't remember anything of the helicopter ride or the drive," he tells me. He spends the next few minutes telling me all about the panini. Clearly it's been a long time since he's enjoyed fresh, crusty bread.

"We'll see you when you get off the plane at Ellington," I remind him. "Just a few more hours."

I send the kids to bed around 9 p.m. hoping they can get a few hours of rest. We need to leave the house by 1 a.m. in order to be on the tarmac when the plane lands. Just after midnight, I roam around the house, flipping on lights and gently pulling arms and legs.

"Uuuhhhh . . . what time is it?" they groggily mumble.

"It's time to get up. We have to leave soon if we're going to get to NASA on time."

"Why does Daddy's flight have to come in so eeeaaarrrlllyyy?" they whine as I remind them to brush their teeth before we leave. While they're slow getting moving, once they get out of bed, I can tell the kids are anxious to see their father. They've all picked out special outfits to wear and carefully packed the bags they'll bring with us when we join Drew in quarantine. All four of them get dressed quickly and the girls take extra time to fix their hair and put on the treasured necklaces Drew gave them before he left, a silver chain with a pendant in the shape of a spacewalking astronaut. I note that even Daniel has chosen a polo shirt with Drew's Expedition 61 mission patch embroidered on the chest. Given Daniel's reserved personality, that's about the biggest outward expression of enthusiasm you can get from him. They joke and banter as we throw our bags into the back and pile into the van. They may be playing it cool, but the kids are clearly excited.

Once again, COVID has made everything about this reunion infinitely more complicated. To maintain quarantine, the kids and I must first drive to Johnson Space Center; once there, we mask up and pile into the government-owned minivan driven by our NASA chaperone. We then make the short, fifteen-minute drive to Ellington Field, where the inside of the NASA hangar is fully lit and as bright as daytime. The kids and I slowly climb out of the van and stretch our legs as we wait for instructions. A few more cars arrive. To my delight and surprise, all six of Drew's and Jessica's astronaut classmates pop out of their cars, including Christina and Nick, who were their ISS crewmates just a few months earlier. I'm thrilled they were allowed to come. While we wait for the plane to arrive, we chat in a big circle, talking loudly to bridge the six feet between us, face masks on.

In the distance a pair of bright lights in the sky turn toward the runway, piercing the dark. Our NASA chaperone tells us the plane is about to land. The kids and I follow her into the hangar, and only moments later the NASA jet taxis from the dark runway into the false daylight of the hangar's LED lights. The window blinds are all down, giving us no hint as to the status of the crew inside. The skilled pilot pulls the jet into the hangar and parks it perfectly in the middle.

Our chaperone encourages us to move forward as the airplane door swings open and the stairs are lowered. Spread out behind us, our astronaut friends and a handful of NASA staff keep a safe distance. The kids huddle together next to me, the younger ones bouncing on their toes in anxious anticipation. Jessica steps out first, her confident and casual gait and big smile making it clear that she feels great. Adjusting back to gravity has apparently been no big deal for her. She waves and says hello before moving off to greet others.

Then there he is in the archway of the jet door. Drew grips the handrail and steps down the short flight of stairs with a hint of hesitancy. When his feet hit the ground, I walk toward him, overcome with the full realization that the mission is finally over. He looks so much better than he did just twenty-four hours earlier. The gray pallor of his skin is gone, replaced with a normal, healthy skin tone. He doesn't look tired or in any kind of pain. He looks healthy and thrilled to see us. He seems a little unsteady on his feet, but that's to be expected as his body adjusts after such a long time in weightlessness. That must have been some panini.

We embrace in a long, tight hug, my face pressed into his neck. My worry and angst dissipate as I wrap my arms around him and can tangibly feel the man who has been only a virtual apparition for so long. His body feels strong and firm under my hands, if just a little wobbly. I pull back to study his face and look into his eyes. He is still a little pale. I notice a few more gray hairs at his temples and see that his last space haircut wasn't the best—he has a few funny tufts of hair sticking up in the back. He looks different to me than when he left, but in a good way. He has the twinkle in his eye of a person who has literally seen the world from a new vantage point and is now wiser and humbler because of it. I'm sure I look different to him too. Like Drew, I've experienced the extraordinary, and I am fundamentally changed because of it. Looking at each other, we laugh at the shared realization that we have crossed the finish line together.

"We did it," he says. "I knew we could do it." We pull the kids in for a giant group hug on the tarmac in front of everyone. As the kids squirm under our communal embrace, I exhale and allow myself the full relief and joy of a safe return.

"We love you," I tell him. "We are so proud of you."

"I am so happy to be home," he replies.

EPILOGUE

April 25, 2020

Drew has been back on Earth for a week. The only people he has had contact with since he got home are me, the kids, and a small team of doctors and scientists wrapped in protective gear who measure and monitor his recovery. All the usual postflight activities that would normally help an astronaut reconnect with their family, friends, and the world in general have been canceled. No meetings, no parties, no visitors. No going to restaurants, church services, friends' houses, or the movies. Our family summer vacation plans and our romantic anniversary trip to Europe have been shelved. Drew's postflight travel around the world with his crewmates is postponed indefinitely. Instead, the six of us are trapped in our house with little to do but stare at one another. We're all a bit sad and disappointed.

"The irony that I went from isolation in space with five people to isolation at home with five people is not lost on me," he says.

"The irony that we went from not living with each other for ten months to being together almost every minute of the day, every day of the week—more than we ever have in our entire married life—is not lost on me," I reply.

So I'm thrilled when the leader of our small group from church calls and tells me to do whatever it takes to get Drew outside our house at exactly 2 p.m. "Don't tell Drew," they say. "A few of us want to drive by and say hello to surprise him."

"He'll love that," I answer. "We'll be waiting!"

"We may have invited a few other people too," they mention in passing, right before quickly hanging up.

I'm jumpy and excited all morning. A celebration of any kind! Human interaction with people not blood related to me! Finally! The late-night skulking into mission control, the jet landing in the dark, the rapid whisking away of the crew to the quarantine facility for days on end with minimal outside interaction—it felt more like a covert operation to sneak a pair of fugitives into the country rather than a celebrated, triumphant return of a successful NASA crew. Every aspect of the return so far has been so muted, so subtle, so anticlimactic.

At the appointed time, I grab Drew's hand and pull him toward the front door. In order to keep the surprise, I haven't told the kids anything either, but they sense something is going on and wander toward us by the front door. In quarantine, any time someone opens the front door and steps out, it's a newsworthy event so they're curious to know why I'm so adamant that Drew join me outside.

"What's going on?" he asks as we step into the sun, noticing the neighbors standing in their driveway on the other side of the street.

He waves and they excitedly wave back. The kids hover behind us on the grass, equally unsure of what's happening.

"A few friends want to welcome you home," I say. "They've missed you."

Reaching the sidewalk, we hear a deep horn blast and turn our heads in unison toward the end of the street, completely unprepared for what comes around the corner.

It starts with a fire engine—lights flashing, siren wailing every few seconds. In between the whoop-whoops of the fire truck, we can hear music, but it's not until the truck turns the corner that we see the pickup truck following closely behind. The pickup is pulling a trailer, on which there's a full rock band, complete with microphones, amplifiers, guitars, and a drum set. On lead vocals is our friend and musician Aric Harding, and the group is jamming out, playing a killer cover of one of Drew's favorite U2 songs with as much enthusiasm as a band opening for Beyoncé at Coachella.

I want to run, I want to hide.
I want to tear down the walls that hold me inside.

Aric and Drew lock eyes as the trailer pulls off to the far side of the street in front of our house so they can continue to rock out while the rest of the parade passes by. Aric has to stop singing for a minute to collect himself. Drew's eyes are wet, and he's holding my hand in a vise grip.

Following the rock band comes a parade of love and support for Drew—a line of cars containing a community of people wanting to show him how welcomed home he truly is.

Our small group.

The entire Boy Scout troop.

NASA friends, fellow astronauts, and their families.

The town mayor and his wife.

Friends from church.

Drew's friends.

My friends.

The kids' friends.

Neighbors and random well-wishers from the community.

They ride in cars, in vans, and in five more fire engines.

Each vehicle is draped with balloons, streamers, and posters that say "Welcome home!" and "We are proud of you!"

Kids and adults alike are hanging out of car windows and standing up through sunroofs, waving, smiling, and singing along with the music as they slowly drive by.

They're wearing NASA shirts and plastic space helmets.

They fire off confetti cannons and throw candy and blast their own music from their car stereos.

"You did it!" they yell to us.

"Congratulations!"

"We love you!"

"Welcome home!"

Over one hundred cars roll past us as we stand stunned on the sidewalk, each vehicle filled with people. As they pass, they reach out their hands toward us, across the passenger seat or out the window, in the universal gesture of "I want to connect with you, if even from a distance."

Drew hasn't stopped holding on to me since we stepped outside. Some people watching assume he must be a little unsteady on his feet, still adjusting to the effects of gravity, but I know better. This overwhelming display of friendship and community is so powerful and unexpected, it threatens to knock Drew off his feet. I know that's how he feels because I feel it too. We cling to each other for support as wave after wave of love washes over us, so strong it threatens to topple us over. It's far better than any standard welcome home party we could have imagined in normal, pre-pandemic days. This unique time has led to the creation of something new, something unique and special on its own, fueled by the human desire—the human need—to connect in any and every way possible. As friends, as a community, as people, even in a really strange, troublesome time where connection is scarce and complicated, we've found a way.

It's not at all what we expected as a grand finale to Drew's mission. It's not a formal ceremony, press interview, or cocktail party with drinks and hors d'oeuvres. Instead, it's a free-spirited, rock 'n' roll, horn-honking, confetti-blasting, raucous testament to the power of embracing the fact that life may be hard, but it can still be good. It's the perfect bookend to this season because it encapsulates so well the unexpected, and yet no less meaningful, way the mission has affected our family. God has used it all—the unfulfilled expectations, the disappointment, the frustration, along with the hope for a better tomorrow, the love of our community, and our pride in finishing the mission well—and created something brand-new, something even better.

An hour later, after the last car honks and drives out of sight, Drew and I wander back inside, still dumbstruck by the gift we've just been given. We stand in the living room for a moment, attempting to regain our emotional equilibrium.

"How do we go back to having a regular day after experiencing that?" I ask him.

"I don't know," he responds. "I think it's impossible."

＊　＊　＊

Here's what I learned that year—the year I sent my husband into outer space, the year of a global pandemic, the year I put hope into practice, found new ways to connect, have fun, relish my freedom, take risks, and lean on others more than I ever thought I could—the year I became stronger than I knew was possible.

Sometimes life is amazing, full of awe and wonder. And sometimes it's full of disappointment and misery. That's okay. That's how life is supposed to be. It's not easy or predictable. Life is a full-blown, knock-your-socks-off adventure story, not a tragedy or a fairy tale. Like any good saga, it's guaranteed to have more ups and downs and twists and turns than you ever could have imagined. And just when you think the story is over, a new chapter begins. God invites us to step into it with him, writing it together as we go. Let's make it a vast epic, full of color and sound and failure and victory and laughter and tears. Let's find a new way to live, embracing it all.

ACKNOWLEDGMENTS

Thank you to the countless people who have supported me, not only on this literary journey, but long before this book was born.

To Annie F. Downs, the catalyst. Who would have guessed that a relatively chance encounter at Johnson Space Center, followed by lunch at Whataburger, would spark not just a book project and everything else that comes with it, but a treasured friendship? Thank you for every big and little thing you've done to advocate for me, guide me, and encourage me. I will be forever grateful.

To my literary agent, Lisa Jackson, along with Sarah Atkinson, Kim Miller, and my entire Tyndale team. You made this all too easy.

To Meredith, who encouraged me to take my first big step. Thank you!

To my dearest friends who found themselves tangled up in my stories: Lisa, Allison, Catie, Ashley, Amber, and Jennifer. Recounting our shenanigans brought tears to my eyes, reminding me how very blessed I am to have friends like you. Thank you for your years of love and friendship.

To my parents, my in-laws, and all my other family and friends—I cannot thank you enough. You endured constant updates about the project, proofread endless pages of material, offered invaluable second opinions, and were always my biggest fans.

Thank you to Daniel, Amelia, Sophia, and Gabriella, who shoulder a burden of service few other children understand and do so with a remarkable level of strength and resiliency. It is a joy to be your mother, and I love you more than anything.

To Drew, my best friend and hero. You promised me a life of adventure, and you continue to deliver! I could never have started or finished this project without your unwavering love and support. Thank you to the ultimate teammate.

And finally, to every military and astronaut spouse who came before me and those who serve alongside me today. Without you, this life of service, sacrifice, and courage would be far more daunting. With you, it is infinitely more rewarding. I am thankful to be counted among you.

Q & A WITH THE AUTHOR

Did you have any idea that this journey would ever become a book?

Never! Over the past ten years or so I started keeping a journal (I use that term loosely—it's more like a document on my computer that I occasionally type some notes into) because life kept throwing things at our family that I knew I'd want to remember in more detail. I speak often to women's groups, so at most, I thought those stories would add interest and humor to my prepared talks. But when the opportunity to write a book presented itself and I began to organize my thoughts and stories into something bigger, I was humbled and thrilled to see that there were some big themes woven throughout the last couple of decades of my life and our family's experience.

What was the writing process like for you?

As an avid reader, I've always had a huge amount of respect for authors, but it's even greater now that I've completed a book myself. The writing process was mentally tough because, at least for me, it required a level of introspection and reflection on past events that was not always comfortable. Because of my personality, I always look forward, sometimes at the expense of reflecting on and learning from my own history. There were days and weeks when I needed to walk away and give my thoughts some time to settle before coming back and trying again. And writing in the midst of a pandemic while all four of my kids were at home wasn't always easy! I had to get a pair of noise-canceling headphones to stay focused.

Your story is definitely one of unique adventure. Did you ever worry you weren't called or equipped for it? Did you ever wrestle with God and wonder if he really wanted you to do it?
Yes! But I tend to be a person who quickly jumps into things with both feet, which means I often find myself in the middle of new projects or experiences before I start asking those questions. It's when I'm knee-deep and things start to get hairy that I start wondering if God actually called me into a new challenge or if it was just my own pride that got me into this predicament. I think most people feel this way at some point in every journey. Looking back, I can see examples of times when God did clearly call me into an adventure that he then equipped me for and other times when I foolishly busted through a window when God had obviously closed a door. But even in the quandaries of my own making, I can see how God ultimately used those experiences for good and equipped me for what I needed to do.

For long stretches of time, you parented solo without easy access to your husband. What has the experience taught you about the challenges full-time single parents face?
As hard or as long as my solo parenting seasons have been, I fully appreciate that they have been temporary. Full-time single parents function on a resiliency and toughness level most of us don't

appreciate. The challenges they face and the hard choices they have to make daily are significant burdens that can really take a physical and mental toll. If my temporary time parenting alone taught me anything, it's that we should do everything we can to support single parents. I was so appreciative any time someone stepped up and offered help without me having to ask, specifically when it came to assisting with the kids or tasks that required more than one adult. From moving furniture and completing home improvement projects to carpooling, helping with driver's ed, or just lending a listening ear, it took a village to raise my kids when I was alone. Whenever we have the opportunity to show compassion and understanding or give tangible help to a single parent, we should.

What do you think is the best way for people to support friends and neighbors who are in a tough season, including single parents, new moms, or spouses of deployed servicemen and women?
While the needs of every person are different, the best advice I have for those who want to help someone is to simply *do something.* Don't wait for them to send you an invitation to help. Don't say, "Call me if you need anything." They probably won't call because to their ears your sincere offer may sound a bit hollow. Instead, say, "I'd like to bring you dinner this week. Which night is best?" or "I'm going to mow your lawn on Tuesday." Offer to watch their kids on Saturday afternoon or bring their child home after school. If you don't live nearby, you can order them a pizza or send a gift card or an encouraging note.

For anyone in a tough season, just knowing that people are thinking of them, praying for them, and offering tangible help in whatever way they can is huge. Even a simple text message is meaningful. And be free with your hugs. When Drew was gone I often went days or even weeks without any meaningful physical contact. Sometimes you just need a good, long hug; a warm arm around your shoulder; or someone to hold your hand.

What did Drew do for fun while in space? Could he bring books and music?

Entertainment is extremely important for astronauts! They can have TV shows and movies uploaded for them to watch on a laptop, which they often do while they exercise or have downtime. Same thing for music. As for reading, physical books are heavy and bulky, so not great for packing into a rocket. Instead, they have digital books and magazines uploaded for them so they can read off an electronic tablet. A few months before Drew's launch, we worked together to write up the list of shows, movies, music, podcasts, magazines, and books he wanted while in space. It was a big task, and we updated it several times during his mission. And while he was gone, if I watched or listened to something I thought Drew would like, I could request that NASA upload it for him so he could watch it too.

Did your parenting style change after nine months apart?

Drew and I have always strongly resonated with the idea of being teammates, and that concept was definitely strengthened while he was in space. The key to thinking like teammates is recognizing that you don't have the same responsibilities or roles and that there are times when one teammate may need to carry more of the load than the other. When it comes to parenting, accepting the temporarily uneven workload while Drew was away was key to preventing me from becoming bitter or resentful and him from becoming detached and despondent.

We knew that as the only parent on the planet, I would be doing all the heavy lifting in the day-to-day parenting of our children. That didn't mean he was unimportant or insignificant, but simply that he wasn't able to be present in the same way I was. So when Drew got home, there was an adjustment period for all of us, just as there had been after his deployments. He had to learn to step in again, I had to remind myself to step back sometimes, and the kids had to remember that there were now two adults to deal with.

We never have a perfectly smooth transition back to "normal," but we have found that reminding each other that we are on the same team helps tremendously in the reintegration process.

How has your marriage changed after nine months apart?
Drew's return from space was so different from any other homecoming we've experienced. Thanks to the pandemic, it was as if he came home and never left the house again! In the past when he'd come back from a long trip or a deployment, he'd leave the house every day for unit meetings, team training, or other activities within just a day or two of his return. That meant we could get used to living with each other again in small doses. Our crew psychologist called it "titrating a return"—doing it a little bit at a time, which was how we assumed we'd handle his return from space as well.

But the pandemic screwed up that plan! With the exception of some physical reconditioning part of each day early on, all of Drew's debriefings were done virtually from home. The kids were also home all day, plus I was working from there, so we were all in the same house almost constantly with nowhere to go. I think Drew and I were both a little nervous about so much uninterrupted time together after such a long time apart. We needed to take walks outside by ourselves once in a while just to have some alone time, but in the end, the fact that we were both at home was great because it gave us blocks of time to talk about his mission. After all, we experienced it together, but in different ways. Having the opportunity to discuss it and then reflect and think about our next steps helped us reconnect faster. It also enhanced our relationship and our teamwork mindset. I don't know if I would recommend the "zero to 60" pandemic reintegration model to every couple, but in this case, it was a positive experience for us.

What questions do you and Drew get asked the most?
By far the two most-asked questions we get are "How do I become an astronaut?" and "How do astronauts go to the bathroom in space?" Drew and I both agree that the best thing you can do to become an astronaut (aside from having the required educational and work experience) is to be a great teammate. After all, if you're going to be trapped in a spaceship for months or years on end with other people, you want them to be selfless and considerate—willing to put others, and the mission, over themselves. It's a concept that has been really valuable to us as a family during the pandemic, but it also applies to life in general. What makes someone a great astronaut also makes that person a great friend/spouse/parent/neighbor/roommate/all-around good person to hang out with, so it's really an important life skill for everyone to work on, even those who never want to go to space.

As for the bathroom question, the simple answer is: suction toilets. Space toilets are equal parts gross and fascinating to learn about. Every astronaut learns how to fix the toilet because it's obviously a key piece of equipment on the ISS.

What is the coolest "space fact" you've learned that most of us don't know?

I've picked up so many random space facts over the years. For example, the exercise bike on the space station doesn't have a seat. Astronauts just clip their feet in and hover over the bike while they pedal! Speaking of feet, the bottoms of astronauts' feet get baby smooth because while in space they aren't using them to walk. Instead they develop calluses on the tops of their feet from hooking them under things to stabilize themselves.

What do you hope your kids have learned from watching you and Drew navigate this mission?

I hope they saw that we stayed committed to each other, were brave, and honored God, even when things were tough or scary. I know that the kids won't fully understand or appreciate much of what they observed—from launch all the way until landing— until they are older. But years from now when they look back, I hope they see two people who embraced adventure together, even when it involved risk and sacrifice, so they could step fully into the opportunities God placed before them.

If you could go into space yourself, would you do it? Why or why not?

That is a question I have asked myself a lot over the past several years. I love the excitement and energy that come with being a part of a dynamic, purposeful team like an astronaut crew. I love facing unique challenges, solving problems, and building new things with people I know and trust. In that way, I think I would really like going to space. Who wouldn't want to be a part of that kind of epic adventure? But at the same time, I really love long, hot showers;

feeling the wind on my face; and sleeping in on weekends. In that way, I think I'm better suited to keeping my feet on the ground.

The public doesn't often hear about astronaut spouses or families. Are you all friends? Do you get together often?

My fellow astro spouses are some of the most accomplished people I know. From teachers and lawyers to doctors, nurses, engineers, stay-at-home parents, military officers, and fighter pilots, they are all equally as impressive and fascinating as astronauts are. We are a small, tightly knit community of friends, and we do gather together on a regular basis to socialize, share information, and celebrate one another. Even after astronauts leave NASA, we see each other at reunions and stay connected on social media. We also build relationships with the astronaut spouses of our international partners, which is a really unique opportunity as well. There is something powerfully universal about the spaceflight experience, no matter what kind of spacecraft it was, whether our spouse launched in 1961 or 2021, or whether they flew for the United States or for a different country. We feel that bond whenever we are together. There are few people on Earth who can relate to what we experience, so we enjoy spending time with one another whenever possible. And during a space mission, connecting with other astro spouses is critical. Much like bonding with my fellow military spouses during deployments was essential to not just surviving but thriving in that season, the support I received from other astro spouses made all the difference during Drew's mission. I could not have done it without them.

DISCUSSION GUIDE

1. How much did you know about NASA and the modern history of space travel prior to reading this book? Were you among those fascinated by space as a child, or who had a formative memory of landmark events like the 1986 *Challenger* or 2003 *Colombia* disaster? If so, explain.

2. As Stacey readies for Drew's launch, the biblical story of Esther runs through her mind. What elements of the story strike a chord with her and why? Have you ever had a defining "for such a time as this" moment?

3. Stacey says: "While we are in the midst of our unique, difficult circumstances . . . God gives each of us the ability to choose the path of either hope or fear. Whether we like it or not, we will live our lives dictated by one or the other, and if we don't make an active decision to choose hope, our default will always be fear" (page 18). Do you agree that hope is an active decision while fear is a default reaction? Why or why not?

4. "Find your people" is a core lesson that Stacey learns through relocations and Drew's deployments. What does this look like for her? In what ways does it look similar or different in your own life? Who are "your people," and what draws you together?

5. Stacey shares about being on both the giving and the receiving end of vulnerability. Think about some times you've cared for others and been cared for. Which was more of a challenge for you and why? What came out of the experience?

6. What are some of the ways Drew and his family stayed connected during the mission? What didn't work out so well, and how did they adapt? What did Stacey and Drew learn about their kids and themselves during this time?

7. Stacey introduces us to the perils of Survival-Me, saying: "My children are watching me, every moment of every day, to see what it means to live a full life. Just because I'm in a challenging season does not mean I should be any less myself. God made me an adventure seeker, a lifelong learner, a risk-taker, and a woman who laughs easily. Switching to autopilot may make life easier today, but I'll pay for it tomorrow with interest. If I don't feed my soul, if I don't remember to laugh and have fun, I am not living a full life" (page 116). How would you complete these sentences:

    a. God made me a _____

    b. If I don't do _____ to feed my own soul, I'm not living a full life.

8. "Why do we accept risk in the dull, inconsequential parts of our lives," Stacey asks, "like driving on the highway at night, climbing a ladder to hang Christmas lights, or eating expired yogurt, but then reject it when it's attached to something new and exciting? Why do we limit ourselves and talk ourselves

out of taking risks?" (pages 160–161). What do you think the answer is?

9. Drew returns from space in the midst of a global pandemic. Do you relate to any aspects of the Morgans' COVID-19 experience? If so, in what way?

10. What takeaways from *The Astronaut's Wife* resonate most with you and why?

NOTES

1. "The Moon: 'A Giant Leap for Mankind,'" *Time* 94, no. 4, July 25, 1969, https://time.com/vault/issue/1969-07-25/page/12/.

2. "Space Shuttle Era," NASA, last updated August 3, 2017, https://www.nasa.gov/mission_pages/shuttle/flyout/index.html; "Space Shuttle Era Facts," NASA, https://www.nasa.gov/pdf/566250main_SHUTTLE%20ERA%20FACTS_040412.pdf.

3. "History and Timeline of the ISS," ISS National Laboratory, https://www.issnationallab.org/about/iss-timeline/.

4. This is not an exact quote, but it is what I remembered when I wrote about this experience in my journal only a few days after the launch.

5. NASA, "Replay: ISS Spacewalk with Nick Hague and Andrew Morgan to Install Int'l Docking Adapter-3," August 21, 2019, https://www.youtube.com/watch?v=SEaXXbAd2wg&t=8695s.

6. Short for "Ground Intravehicular"

7. David Bowie, "Space Oddity," 1969 © Sony/ATV Music Publishing LLC, BMG Rights Management, Tintoretto Music.

8. United States Parachute Association, "How Safe Is Skydiving?," https://uspa.org/Discover/FAQs/Safety.

9. As NASA explains, "Humanity's only orbital laboratory, the space station, orbits the Earth [in] about 90 minutes or about 16 times every 24 hours." "Seeing Our Moon from the Space Station," NASA web page, February 3, 2021, https://www.nasa.gov/image-feature/seeing-our-moon-from-the-space-station.

ABOUT THE AUTHOR

STACEY MORGAN is always ready with a funny or thoughtful story from her own life; whether it be holding down the home front during Special Forces military deployments, carpooling, working for the Smithsonian, skydiving, teaching her teens to drive, taking roller-skating lessons, or blasting her husband into outer space.

A women's ministry leader for over fifteen years, Stacey is an executive leadership coach for MOPS International, a nonprofit focused on the unique needs of mothers around the world. She is married to Army colonel and NASA astronaut Drew Morgan. They have four children, ranging from elementary to high school age. When she's not writing or speaking at women's events, she's watching historical dramas, reading a good mystery novel, or planning her next adventure. Learn more about Stacey at StaceyMorgan2000.com or theastronautswife.com.